Essential Histories

# The Wars of
# Alexander the Great
336–323 BC

Essential Histories

# The Wars of Alexander the Great

336–323 BC

Waldemar Heckel

OSPREY
PUBLISHING

First published in Great Britain in 2002 by Osprey Publishing,
Elms Court, Chapel Way, Botley, Oxford OX2 9LP, UK
Email: info@ospreypublishing.com

ISBN 1 84176 473 6

Editor: Rebecca Cullen
Design: Ken Vail Graphic Design, Cambridge, UK
Cartography by The Map Studio
Index by David Worthington
Picture research by Image Select International
Origination by Grasmere Digital Imaging, Leeds, UK
Printed and bound in China by L. Rex Printing Company Ltd.

02  03  04  05  06    10  9  8  7  6  5  4  3  2  1

For a complete list of titles available from Osprey Publishing
please contact:

Osprey Direct UK, PO Box 140,
Wellingborough, Northants, NN8 2FA, UK.
Email: info@ospreydirect.co.uk

Osprey Direct USA, c/o MBI Publishing,
PO Box 1, 729 Prospect Ave,
Osceola, WI 54020, USA.
Email: info@ospreydirectusa.com

**www.ospreypublishing.com**

# Contents

# Introduction

The conquests of Alexander the Great form a watershed between the world of the Greek city-state (*polis*) and the so-called Hellenistic world, the eastern kingdoms, where Alexander's successors applied a veneer of Greek culture and administration to a barbarian world. These ancient Near Eastern territories had always been the battleground between eastern and western civilisations, and would continue to be so well beyond the chronological confines of the ancient world.

Western contact with the Near East had begun in the Bronze Age, in Hittite Asia Minor, in the Orontes valley of Syria and in the Nile delta of Egypt. The spectacular frescoes and other artefacts of the prehistoric civilisations of the Aegean depict contact, friendly and hostile, between foreigners and Mycenaean–Minoan 'Greeks'. Even after the fall of Troy ended what the historian Herodotus regarded as the first great struggle between east and west, and after the collapse of the Bronze Age civilisations – under circumstances that are still not clear – new waves of Greek migrants splashed against the shores of Asia Minor. From there, they spread to the Black Sea coast and the Levant, and eventually to the west as well.

By the sixth century BC, however, Greek settlements in Asia Minor became subject to the authority of the Lydians. This kingdom had allied itself with the Medes, who ruled the Persians from Ecbatana (modern Hamadan) until they were overthrown by Cyrus the Great. Croesus, whose name is synonymous with fabulous wealth, was the last of the Lydian rulers and, in 548/7, he raised an army against the Persian upstart, misled by Greek oracles into thinking that he would acquire a greater empire. After an indecisive battle near the Halys, the Lydian troops disbanded, as was their practice – for it was not customary to wage war over the winter months – but Cyrus brought his Persians up to the walls of Sardis, seized its citadel and put Croesus to death. (Greek tradition was embarrassed by the oracle's deception and maintained that Apollo intervened at the last minute, saving Croesus from the flames and transporting him to an idyllic world.)

Between 547 and 540 Cyrus's generals subdued coastal Asia Minor, while he turned his attention to the Elamites and Babylonians. By the end of the century, the Achaemenids ruled an empire that extended from the Indus to the Aegean and from Samarkand to the first cataracts of the Nile. The title 'King of Kings' was thus no empty boast.

Marble head of Alexander. (Greek Ministry of Culture)

Persian domination of Greek Asia Minor threatened the city-states of the peninsula to the west, as well as the islands that lay in between. In 513 Darius I crossed the Hellespont (Dardanelles), the narrow strait that separates the Gallipoli peninsula of Europe from what is today Asiatic Turkey. Portions of Thrace were annexed and administered as the Persian satrapy of Skudra, and at some point thereafter the Persians received the submission of Macedon. Even the isolationist states to the south, in particular Sparta, were forced to take notice.

The Athenians and the Eretrians of Euboea had aided a rebellion by the Ionians,

The tomb of Cyrus the Great, the founder of the Persian Empire (d. 530 BC). Alexander had Poulamachos, a Macedonian, impaled for desecrating the tomb. (TRIP)

descendants, the Gortyae, fought Alexander at Gaugamela. Then Datis landed on Athenian soil at Marathon; however, contrary to expectation, a predominantly Athenian force defeated the Persian army.

The Athenian victory provided an immense boost to Greek confidence, which would be put to the test ten years later, when Darius' son and successor, Xerxes, came dangerously close to defeating a coalition of Greeks and adding the lower Balkans to the Persian Empire. Only the great naval victory at Salamis (summer 480) prevented the Persian juggernaut from crushing all resistance in Greece. That victory hastened the retreat of Xerxes with the bulk of his army; those who remained under Mardonius were dealt the decisive blow on the battlefield of Plataea in 479.

The ill-fated expedition of Xerxes resulted in strained but stable relations between Greece and Persia, a balance of power that in some respects resembled the Cold War of the twentieth century. The Greek world, however, was itself divided and polarised, with the Spartans exercising hegemony over the Peloponnesian League as a counterweight to Athens, which, under the guise of liberating the Hellenes from Persia, had converted the Delian League – originally, a confederacy of autonomous allies – into an empire. By the middle of the fifth century, Athens was reaping the financial benefits of the incoming tribute and unashamedly extolling the virtues of 'power politics'. The inevitable clash of

a futile (as it turned out) attempt to throw off the Persian yoke (499/498–494/493). Victorious over the rebels, Darius launched a punitive campaign against their supporters: in 490 his general, Datis, crossed the Aegean and destroyed the city of the Eretrians, many of whom were subsequently enslaved in the heart of the Persian Empire – their

*Demosthenes on Persia*
'I consider the Great King to be the common enemy of all the Greeks ... Nor do I see the Greeks having a common friendship with one another, but some trust the King more than they do some of their own [race].'
Demosthenes 14.3

## The extent and composition of the Persian Empire

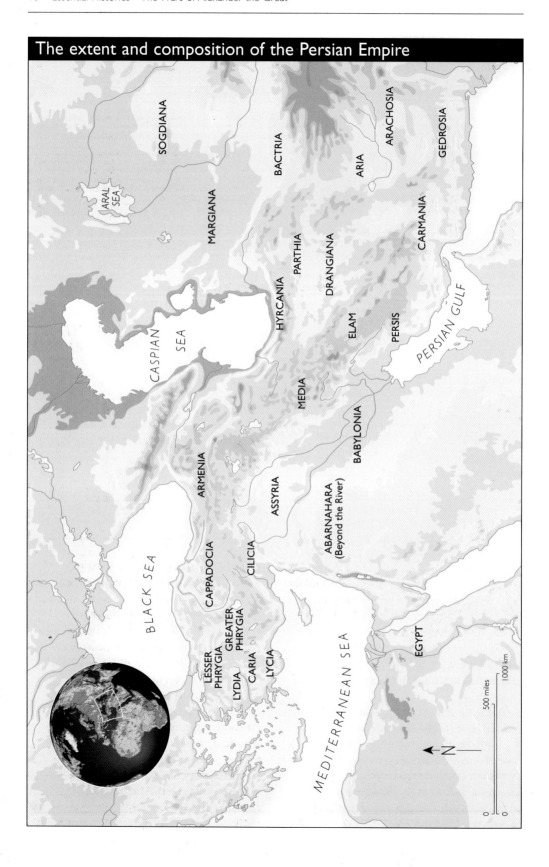

## The Marathon campaign, 490 BC

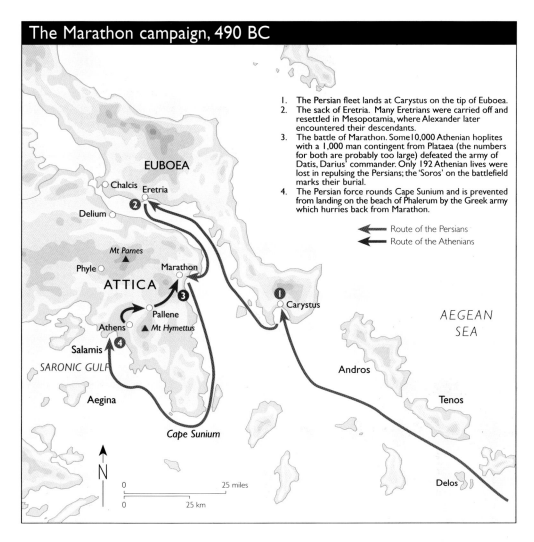

1. The Persian fleet lands at Carystus on the tip of Euboea.
2. The sack of Eretria. Many Eretrians were carried off and resettled in Mesopotamia, where Alexander later encountered their descendants.
3. The battle of Marathon. Some 10,000 Athenian hoplites with a 1,000 man contingent from Plataea (the numbers for both are probably too large) defeated the army of Datis, Darius' commander. Only 192 Athenian lives were lost in repulsing the Persians; the 'Soros' on the battlefield marks their burial.
4. The Persian force rounds Cape Sunium and is prevented from landing on the beach of Phalerum by the Greek army which hurries back from Marathon.

← Route of the Persians
← Route of the Athenians

EUBOEA
Chalcis ○  Eretria
Delium ○
Mt Parnes ▲
Phyle ○      Marathon ○
ATTICA
Pallene ○
Athens ○  ▲ Mt Hymettus
Salamis
SARONIC GULF
Aegina
Cape Sunium
Carystus ○
AEGEAN SEA
Andros
Tenos
Delos

N
0        25 miles
0     25 km

Greek powers took place between 431 and 404 and was known as the Peloponnesian War (see *The Peloponnesian War* in this series). When it was over, the Athenian Empire existed no more and the gradual decline of the Greek city-states through internecine warfare set the stage for the emergence of a great power in the north: the kingdom of Macedon.

The struggle for hegemony amongst the city-states of Sparta, Thebes and Athens made it clear that Greek unity – the elusive concept of Panhellenism – was something that could not be achieved peacefully, through negotiation or commitment to a greater purpose; rather it was something to be imposed from outside. Earlier the Greeks

had closed ranks in order to resist the common enemy, Persia. But when the threat receded, the Hellenic League dissolved and the political horizons of the Greeks narrowed. Certain intellectuals nevertheless promoted the concept of Panhellenism, even if it meant the forcible unification of the city-states. When Philip achieved this, by means of his victory at Chaeronea and the creation of the League of Corinth, he attempted to renew Panhellenic vigour by reminding the Greeks of the 'common enemy', the Persians.

The concept of a war of vengeance was, however, a hard sell. Although some appealed directly to Philip to bring about the unification of Greece and lead it against

Persia, others, like Demosthenes, who criticised the interference of the Persian King in Greek affairs, espoused Panhellenism only if it could be accomplished under Athenian leadership or for Athenian benefit. And there were like-minded politicians in the other *poleis* who favoured unity under the hegemony of their own states. In the face of Macedonian imperialism, Demosthenes was content – at least, according to his accusers – to accept Persian money to resist Philip and Alexander.

# Chronology

# The decline of the city-states and the rise of Macedon

## Decline of the Greek city-states

The victory of Sparta in the Peloponnesian War (431–404 BC) and the destruction of the Athenian Empire ended the balance of power in the Greek world. Sparta emerged as an oppressive and unimaginative master. Nevertheless, the price of victory had been great and domination of Greece made demands on Sparta that she could not easily meet. Sparta was notoriously short of manpower and the needs of empire – maintaining garrisons and fleets, and providing Spartiate officials abroad – strained her resources and undermined the simple but effective socio-economic basis of the state and its military power. Newly enfranchised helots (state slaves) performed garrison duty, and wealth infiltrated Spartan society; personal wealth and the use of gold and silver had been banned by the legendary lawgiver Lycurgus.

But the problems were not only domestic. Hostility to Spartan power, which was exercised in a ruthless and often corrupt manner, led to a coalition of Thebes, Corinth, Argos and a resurgent Athens against the new masters of Greece. Although Sparta withstood this initial test, which is referred to as the Corinthian War (394–387/386), the bitter confrontations of this war were the forerunners of a life-and-death struggle that would see the brief emergence of Thebes as the dominant hoplite power.

The famous Theban wedge began as a defensive measure in 394. Soon, however, it became clear that it had tremendous offensive potential and, as a result of the successful execution of Theban tactics by the renowned Sacred Band, Thebes replaced Sparta as the leader of Greece, at least on land. Sparta's defeat at Theban hands in the battle of Leuctra (371) was catastrophic and it was followed by Theban invasions of the Peloponnese, the foundation of Megalopolis as a check on Spartan activities in the south, and the liberation of Messenia, which had hitherto provided Sparta's helots and its economic underpinnings.

> *The Thebans' comment on the nature of Spartan imperialism*
>
> 'Now we are all aware, men of Athens, that you would like to get back the empire which you used to have. Surely this is more likely to happen if you go to the help of all victims of Spartan injustice ... In the war with you [these states], at the urgent entreaties of Sparta, took their share in all the hardships and dangers and expense; but when the Spartans had achieved their object, did they ever get any share of the power or glory or money that was won? Far from it. The Spartans, now that things have gone well for them, think it perfectly proper to set up their own helots as governors, and meanwhile treat their free allies as though they were slaves ... What they gave them was not freedom but a double measure of servitude.
>
> This arrogant dominion of Sparta is easier to destroy: ... the Spartans, few in number themselves, are greedily dominating people who are many times as numerous as they and also just as well armed.'
>
> Xenophon, *Hellenica* 3.5.10–15 (Rex Warner trans., Penguin)

## Greek encounters with Persia

These convulsions in central and southern Greece must be viewed against the

Monument commemorating the Theban victory over Sparta at Leuctra (371 BC). The victory was attributable to the Theban wedge and the courage of the Sacred Band. For Sparta the defeat was staggering, and the Theban general Epamonidas exploited Spartan weakness by invading Peloponnesus, establishing the city of Megalopolis and freeing the Messenians. Theban power came to an abrupt end at Chaeronea in 338 BC, and three years later the city was destroyed by Alexander. (Photo by the author)

ever-present backdrop of the Persian Empire. In the middle of the Peloponnesian War – during an unstable period known, misleadingly, as the Peace of Nicias – the Athenians had suffered a devastating defeat in Sicily. For a state that was ringed with enemies, the collapse of the army in the west had much the same effect as Napoleon's and Hitler's disastrous Russian campaigns. For the subject states of the empire, it was the signal for rebellion, and defections occurred on a grand scale.

Economically battered and militarily shaken, Athens now resumed the war against

Sparta, which at the same time had found a paymaster in the Persian King. Although Athens had made peace with Artaxerxes I – the infamous and much disputed Peace of Callias (449) – this agreement needed to be renewed, and there had apparently not been a formal agreement with Artaxerxes' successor, Darius II (424–403). Darius at first allowed his satraps to distribute funds to Sparta and her allies in the hope of recovering the Greek coastal cities.

The compact with Persia that followed, while militarily expedient, was politically harmful to Sparta's reputation amongst the Greeks. For, in the struggle to defeat Athens, which had once espoused the liberty of the Hellenes, Sparta was agreeing to hand back Greek city-states in Asia Minor to Persia. In 407, Darius sent a younger son, Cyrus, to supply the Spartans with the resources to defeat their enemies. In the process, Cyrus developed a strong bond of friendship with the Spartan admiral Lysander. The latter had political ambitions at home, and the former was eager to bring about a Peloponnesian victory in the war so that he could, in the near future, draw upon their soldiery, which he regarded as the best in the ancient world.

The health of Darius II was clearly failing, and the heir to the throne was Cyrus's elder brother, Artaxerxes (II). He appears to have been a rather lethargic man, already approaching middle age. A faction at court, encouraged by the efforts of the queen mother, sought to win the kingship for Cyrus. But, in order to challenge his brother, Cyrus would need a military edge. And this, he believed, could be supplied by a Greek mercenary army. Darius died soon after the collapse of Athens, and in 402/401, Cyrus set in motion his scheme to overthrow Artaxerxes. A force of some 11,000 mercenaries – they were to become known (after some defections and casualties) as the 'Ten Thousand' – accompanied a vastly greater barbarian force from Lydia to Mesopotamia.

Not far from Babylon, at a place called Cunaxa, the armies of the feuding brothers met. Although the Greeks won an easy victory against the barbarians stationed opposite them, the effort was for naught, since Cyrus himself was killed in an attack on his brother in the centre of the line. Struck under the eye with a javelin, Cyrus fell, and with him collapsed the dream for the fulfilment of which an army had struggled against distance and difficult terrain, and ultimately a vastly more numerous enemy. But it was not entirely in vain, at least as a lesson to the Greeks: for the ease with which a relatively mobile and efficient army could strike at the heart of the empire exposed the weaknesses of Achaemenid Persia. One of the Greeks who participated in the campaign, Xenophon, wrote a colourful account of the adventure, which made delightful reading for Greek schoolboys. It was almost certainly read by Alexander in his youth, and its lessons did not elude him.

In the meantime, Athens too had attempted to revive its maritime power, creating the Second Athenian League. But this fell far short of the Delian League of the fifth century, for the member states were wary of Athenian imperialistic ambitions and

*Xenophon's observations on the nature of the Persian Empire*

'Generally speaking, it was obvious that Cyrus was pressing on all the way with no pause except when he halted for provisions or some other necessity. He thought that the quicker he arrived the more unprepared would be the King when he engaged him, and the slower he went, the greater would be the army that the King could get together. Indeed, an intelligent observer of the King's empire would form the following estimate: it is strong in respect of the extent of territory and numbers of inhabitants; but it is weak in respect of its lengthened communications and the dispersal of its forces, that is, if one can attack with speed.'
Xenophon, *Anabasis* 1.5.9 (Rex Warner trans., Penguin)

the Athenians themselves incapable of asserting their domination by force. In the event, it mattered little, since the debilitating wars of the city-states to the south had diverted Greek attention from the growing danger in the north.

## The rise of Macedon

The northern kingdom of Macedon was benefiting from a union of the lower region that formed around the Axius river and the shoreline of the Thermaic Gulf with that of the mountain cantons of Upper Macedonia – Elimea, Orestis, Tymphaea and others.

During the Persian Wars, Macedon had been a vassal kingdom of the Persian Empire, and its king, Alexander Philhellene – despite his nickname, which means 'friend of the Greeks' – had acted primarily in his own interests. He had dissuaded a Greek expeditionary force from occupying the Vale of Tempe, which separated Macedonia from Thessaly, for he did not want Xerxes' large army bottled up in Macedonia, where it would be a drain on the kingdom's resources. Later he advised the Athenians to accept the reality of Persian power and surrender to Xerxes. This, of course, they decided not to do.

Alexander's son Perdiccas II ruled during the Peloponnesian War and maintained himself and the kingdom by vacillating between support of Sparta and Athens, according to the threat that each posed and the changing fortunes of the war. By the end of the century, Archelaus (the son of Perdiccas II) had begun to strengthen the kingdom: new roads were created and an effort was made to import Greek culture from the south. Indeed, the playwright Euripides died in Macedonia, where he had written his gruesome tragedy *The Bacchae*. But Archelaus did not live to fulfil his ambitions, succumbing as so many Macedonians did to an assassin's dagger.

The death of Archelaus was followed by a succession of ephemeral rulers until Amyntas III re-established a measure of stability. Nevertheless the kingdom was constantly threatened by the Illyrians to the west and the imperialistic (or, at least, hegemonic) tendencies of the Athenians and Thebans. By the queen Eurydice, Amyntas had three sons, all destined to rule. Alexander II held the throne only briefly (369–368) before he was murdered. A brother-in-law, Ptolemy of Alorus, then served as regent for the under-aged Perdiccas III, until he too was assassinated in 365. Perdiccas was now master of his own house and throne, but the kingdom continued to be threatened by the Illyrians to the west, and in 360/359 these destroyed the Macedonian army, leaving Perdiccas dead on the battlefield and only a child (Amyntas) as heir to the throne.

During the reign of his brothers, the youngest son, Philip, had spent some time as a hostage in Thebes, at that time the most powerful military state in Greece. Here he had witnessed the Theban infantry reforms and had given thought to applying the lessons to the Macedonian army. Hence, when the emergency created by the Illyrian disaster of 360/359 brought him to power, as regent for Amyntas IV, Philip knew not only what to do but how to do it. Indeed, he dealt with the crisis so effectively – combining military action with diplomacy, or even duplicity – that the claims of Amyntas were swept aside. It was Philip's reforms that made the army invincible: little did he realise that, while he was struggling to ensure Macedon's survival, he was training and organising an army of world conquerors.

Philip rapidly mastered northern Thessaly, with its chief town of Larisa, and sealed his political gains by marrying Philinna, a woman of the ruling family. The Phocians

*A wonderful feat of surgery*
 'Critobulus enjoys great celebrity for having removed the arrow from Philip's eye and ensuring that the loss of the eye did not leave his face deformed.'
Pliny, *Natural History* 7.37 (J. C. Yardley trans.)

## Xerxes' invasion of Greece

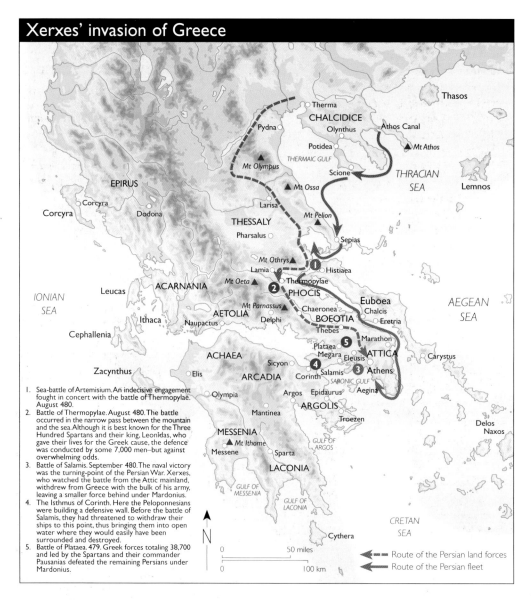

1. Sea-battle of Artemisium. An indecisive engagement fought in concert with the battle of Thermopylae. August 480.
2. Battle of Thermopylae. August 480. The battle occurred in the narrow pass between the mountain and the sea. Although it is best known for the Three Hundred Spartans and their king, Leonidas, who gave their lives for the Greek cause, the defence was conducted by some 7,000 men—but against overwhelming odds.
3. Battle of Salamis. September 480. The naval victory was the turning-point of the Persian War. Xerxes, who watched the battle from the Attic mainland, withdrew from Greece with the bulk of his army, leaving a smaller force behind under Mardonius.
4. The Isthmus of Corinth. Here the Peloponnesians were building a defensive wall. Before the battle of Salamis, they had threatened to withdraw their ships to this point, thus bringing them into open water where they would easily have been surrounded and destroyed.
5. Battle of Plataea. 479. Greek forces totaling 38,700 and led by the Spartans and their commander Pausanias defeated the remaining Persians under Mardonius.

◄━ ━ Route of the Persian land forces
◄━━ Route of the Persian fleet

had plundered the treasures of Delphi in order to buy mercenaries, and the inability of the Thessalians and the Thebans to deal with them cast Philip in the role of the god's champion. After his victory at the Crocus Field in 353, his men wore laurel wreaths on their heads, symbolising their service to Apollo. By 346, by the terms of the Peace of Philocrates, Philip had made himself master of northern Greece. He spoke for Thessaly and he held the deciding votes of the Amphictyonic Council that controlled Delphi.

For a while, Philip directed his attention to the north-east, to the Thraceward area and Byzantium. But in 338, he crushed the combined armies of Athens and Thebes at Chaeronea, and was able to impose a settlement on Greece, through the creation of the League of Corinth, which recognised him as its leader (*hegemon*). The foreign policy of the Greeks was securely in his hands, but Philip's greatest challenges were to come from his own kingdom; indeed, from his own household.

*Alexander relates Philip's achievements*

'Philip found you a tribe of impoverished vagabonds, most of you dressed in skins, feeding a few sheep on the hills and fighting, feebly enough, to keep them from your neighbours – Thracians, Triballians and Illyrians. He gave you cloaks to wear instead of skins; he brought you down from the hills into the plains; he taught you to fight on equal terms with the enemy on your borders, till you knew that your safety lay not, as once, in your mountain strongholds, but in your own valour. He made you city-dwellers; he brought you law; he civilized you ... Thessaly, so long your bugbear and your dread, he subjected to your rule, and by humbling the Phocians he made the narrow and difficult path into Greece a broad and easy road. The men of Athens and Thebes, who for years had kept watching for their moment to strike us down, he brought so low – and by this time I myself was working at my father's side – that they who once exacted from us either our money or our obedience, now, in their turn, looked to us as the means of their salvation.' Arrian 7.9 (A. de Sélincourt trans., Penguin)

Medallion showing the head of Philip II. The fact that the left side of his face is shown may be significant: Philip was struck by an arrow in the right eye during the siege of Methone in 354 BC. (Archaeological Museum of Thessaloniki)

Remains of the Temple of Apollo at Delphi. The Pythia,
the priestess of the god, declared that Alexander would
be invincible. (Author's collection)

The lion of Chaeronea, a monument to the Greeks
who fell at Chaeronea in 338 BC fighting Philip II.
(Author's collection)

# The Persians, the Macedonians and allied troops

## The Persians

From the time of Darius I (521–486), the Persian Empire was divided administratively into 20 provinces known as satrapies, each governed by a satrap – at least, such was the Greek approximation of *khshathrapavan*, a word that is Median in origin and appears to have meant 'protector of the realm'. These satrapies were assessed an annual tribute that ranged from a low of 170 talents of Euboean silver paid by the dwellers of the Hindu Kush region to a staggering 4,680 talents from the neighbouring Indians. (It is pointless to attempt a conversion of ancient into modern values, but it is worth noting that in the late stages of the Peloponnesian War, i.e. about 80 years before Alexander's invasion, 1 talent was sufficient to maintain a trireme, with its complement of 200 men, for a month.) Sums collected in excess of these amounts were presumably for the satraps' personal use.

In addition to the satraps of these 20 provinces, there were rulers of smaller administrative units known to the Greeks as hyparchs (*hyparchoi*), but the use of terminology is often inconsistent in Greek sources and the titles 'satrap' and 'hyparch' are sometimes used interchangeably. Both can be found commanding regionally recruited troops.

The Persian army was composed primarily of satrapal levies, each of the Achaemenid provinces providing troops in accordance with wealth and population. These troops were then divided into units based on tens. Herodotus and Xenophon speak regularly of myriads and chiliarchies, units of 10,000 and 1,000, which the Persians themselves called *baivaraba* and *hazaraba*. Each *baivarabam* had its *baivarpatish* ('myriarch'); and there was a *hazarapatish* ('chiliarch') for every *hazarabam*,

which in turn was subdivided into ten groups of 100 (*sataba*), and these into ten units of ten (*dathaba*). These were, in reality, only nominal strengths, and thus we can explain, at least in part, the wildly exaggerated numbers of Persians in the Greek sources, especially in Herodotus' account of the Persian Wars.

One unit, however, did maintain its full strength of 10,000 and hence was known as the 'Immortals'. This unit formed the elite – men selected for their physical excellence and their valour – and appears to have included a contingent of 1,000 spear-bearers, who followed the King's chariot. In addition to these came the King's special guard of spearmen, known from the golden apples that constituted their spearbutts as *melophoroi* or 'apple-bearers'. These also numbered 1,000 and preceded the King's chariot in the royal procession. Similarly, the King was accompanied by units of 1,000 and 10,000 cavalry.

When Alexander crossed to Asia, Darius III had only recently become king as a result of the convulsions at the Achaemenid court. The ruthless Artaxerxes III Ochus had elevated to positions of great power at the court – he was *hazarapatish* or chiliarch – and in the army, a eunuch by the name of Bagoas. In 338 BC, however, Bagoas murdered first Ochus, and then his sons. Hence, the kingship devolved upon a certain

The Persian Immortals were the elite troops. Their name derives from the fact that their numbers were never allowed to dip below 10,000. Nineteenth - century chromolithograph of the frieze at Susa. (ARPL)

Artashata, whom Greek writers (for reasons that are unclear to us) called Codomannus, and who took the dynastic name Darius (III). Unlike the sons of Ochus, Darius was a mature individual, already in his early forties, and an experienced warrior – he had defeated a Cadusian champion in single combat – who was wise to the machinations of Bagoas and forced him to drink his own poison. When he turned his attention to the Macedonian invaders, he had only just returned from suppressing a fresh uprising in Egypt.

---

*The Royal Procession of the Persians*

' ... in front, on silver altars, was carried the fire which the Persians called sacred and eternal. Next came the Magi, singing the traditional hymn, and they were followed by 365 young men in scarlet cloaks, their number equalling the days of the year. Then came the chariot consecrated to Jupiter [Ahura-Mazda], drawn by white horses, followed by a horse of extraordinary size, which the Persians called "the Sun's horse". Those driving the horses were equipped with golden whips and white robes ... and these were followed by the cavalry of 12 nations of different cultures, variously armed. Next in line were the soldiers whom the Persians called the "Immortals", 10,000 in number ... After a short interval came the 15,000 men known as "the King's kinsmen" ... The column next to these comprised the so-called *Doryphoroe*, ... and these preceded the royal chariot on which rode the King himself ... 10,000 spearmen carrying lances chased with silver and tipped with gold followed the King's chariot, and to the right and left he was attended by some 200 of his most noble relatives. At the end of the column came 30,000 foot-soldiers followed by 400 of the King's horses.'

Quintus Curtius Rufus, *The History of Alexander* 3.3.9–21

---

# The Macedonians

Macedon, by contrast, was the product of a union of Upper and Lower Macedonia, which had been completed in the time of Philip II and to which were added new cities containing new – that is, naturalised – citizens. Several of Alexander's closest friends (*hetairoi*) belonged to the latter group: Nearchus and the sons of Larichus, Laomedon and Erigyius, in particular. Generally speaking, the country was not highly urbanised and most were herdsmen; the state did not have the material for a citizen hoplite army, since most lacked the resources from which to supply themselves with hoplite armour. But Macedonia had a large and robust population, which, if it could be armed cheaply and effectively, could prove too much for its neighbours.

Originally, the core of the Macedonian military was the cavalry, particularly the nobility that formed the king's guard and rode into battle with him as his *comitatus*. Here we first encounter the term *hetairoi*, 'companions' (or 'friends'). Philip appears to have formed an élite battalion of infantry, which he named his 'foot-companions' (*pezhetairoi*). Later the name came to mean the Macedonian infantry in general – that is, the territorial levies, many of them from the Upper Macedonian cantons of Elimeia, Lyncus, Orestis and Tymphaea. The élite foot-guard now became known as the *hypaspistai* or 'shield-bearers', and even these were separate from a group of noble guards described variously as the 'royal hypaspists' or the *agema*.

In the army that followed Alexander to Asia there were 9,000 *pezhetairoi*, dispersed among six brigades (*taxeis*) – each *taxis* comprised 1,500 men – and 3,000 hypaspists. Although some have regarded the hypaspists as more lightly armed than the *pezhetairoi*, the truth is that they were identically armed and only the basis of recruitment was different.

The weapon that distinguished the Macedonian infantryman or phalangite was known as the *sarissa*, a hardwood lance

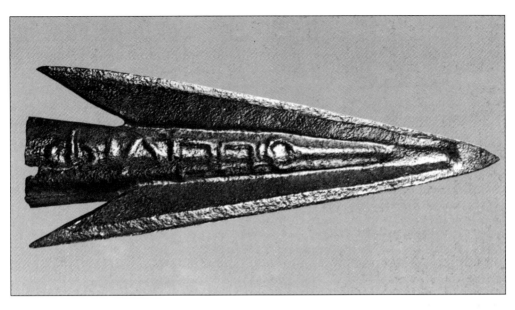

Arrowhead. This one bears the name of Philip. (Archaeological Museum of Thessaloniki)

(often cornel wood) with a metal point and butt-spike. This ranged in length from 15 to 18ft (4.5–5.5m), though longer ones seem to have come into use, and weighed about 14lb (6kg). Since it required two hands to wield, the shield, about 2ft (0.6m) in diameter, was either suspended from the neck, thus rendering the breastplate virtually superfluous, or else attached by means of a sling to the upper arm. The helmet was that of the 'Phrygian' style, worn also by cavalrymen, though the latter are often depicted sporting the so-called Boeotian helmet.

The Macedonian cavalry, known as the Companion Cavalry, was subdivided into squadrons called *ilai*. The strength of an *ile* was probably about 200, though the Royal Squadron (*ile basilike*) comprised 300 men. Eight *ile* of Companions were supplemented by four *ilai* of scouts (*prodromoi*) or sarissa-bearers (*sarissophoroi*) and one of Paeonians. Whereas the Companions were generally armed with the cavalryman's spear (*xyston*), the *sarissophoroi*, as their name implies, wielded the cavalry *sarissa*, a shorter version of the infantryman's lance, probably in the 12–14ft (3.5–4.25m) range, weighing about 4½lb (2kg).

## Allied troops

Both Macedonians and Persians made extensive use of Greek hoplites, while the Macedonians also employed Greek cavalry. But the numbers of Greeks in the Persian army were substantially larger – an embarrassing statistic for Alexander, whose propaganda had attempted to sell his campaign as a Panhellenic war, fought for the good and the pride of all Greeks against a hated enemy.

In Alexander's army, the Thessalian cavalry equalled in strength the Macedonian Companions (1,800–2,000) and fought on the left wing under the general command of Parmenion; but since Thessaly belonged to the political orbit of Macedon and Alexander was the *archon* of the Thessalian League, these troops must be regarded as distinct from those of the 'allies'. Nevertheless, it is worth noting that, once the Panhellenic phase of the conquest was declared over, the Thessalians were allowed to return home, though they sold their horses and returned on foot.

Other allied horsemen are attested, including Peloponnesian horse, Thracians and mercenary cavalry. An inscription from Orchomenus records the names of local cavalrymen who served with Alexander. In 334, Alexander led 7,000 allies and

# The extent of Macedonia

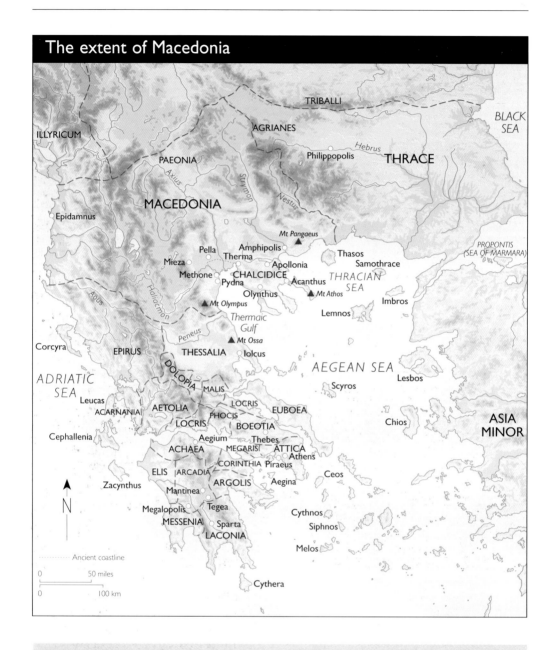

Bronze greaves from Tomb II at Vergina, believed by many scholars to have belonged to Philip II, the father of Alexander the Great. Note the mismatched pair. (Archaeological Museum of Thessaloniki)

5,000 mercenary infantry to Asia, and there was a steady flow of reinforcements throughout the campaign, but also large numbers of Greeks deposited throughout the empire as garrison troops. At the time of Alexander's death, some 10,000 in the Upper Satrapies were planning to abandon their posts and return to Greece, something they had previously attempted upon hearing the false news of the King's death in 325.

The Persians, of course, employed large numbers of Greek mercenaries: 20,000 are attested at the Granicus, and 30,000 at Issus. Captured Greeks were, however, sent by Alexander to hard-labour camps, and it was only with difficulty that their countrymen secured their release. Even when Darius was fleeing south of the Caspian, shortly before his murder at the hands of Nabarzanes and Bessus, significant numbers of Greek mercenaries remained with him, commanded by Patron the Phocian and Glaucus of Aetolia. Eventually these orphaned mercenaries were forced to place themselves at Alexander's mercy.

# Alexander's rise to power

## The assassination of Philip

The outbreak of the Macedonian war of conquest was in fact a two-part process, the first arrested by the assassination of its initiator, Philip II. Once he had crushed Greek resistance at Chaeronea in late summer 338, Philip forged an alliance of city-states, known, after the place where its council met, as the League of Corinth. This convened for the first time in spring 337, elected Philip as its military leader (*hegemon*) and laid the foundations for a Panhellenic expedition against Persia.

What Philip's exact aims were, in terms of territorial acquisition, are not clear. Many suppose that he would have contented himself, initially at least, with the liberation of Asia Minor. This would certainly have been in keeping with Philip's practices in the past. From the time that he overcame internal opposition and secured his borders against barbarian incursions, Philip expanded slowly and cautiously over a period of almost 20 years. Unlike Alexander, whose practice it was to conquer first and consolidate later – and, indeed, 'later' never came in some cases – Philip was content to acquire territory systematically, without overextending Macedonian power.

But Philip's conquests were pre-empted by assassination, and the stability of the kingdom was disrupted by an ill-advised marriage. Macedonian kings, at least from the time of Persian influence in the region (after 513), were polygamous, and Philip married for the seventh time in October 337. The bride was a teenager of aristocratic Macedonian background – most of Philip's brides had, in fact, been foreigners – but the union was the result of a love affair rather than politics. Indeed, Philip was experiencing what we would call a 'mid-life crisis', and the attractions of the young Cleopatra were a pleasant diversion from the affairs of state and the demands of his shrewish queen, Olympias, the mother of Alexander the Great. Philip's infatuation blinded him to both the political expectations of his new wife's family and the resentment of his son and heir.

At the wedding-feast, Cleopatra's uncle, Attalus, had toasted the marriage with the tactless prayer that it should produce 'legitimate' heirs to the Macedonian throne. Alexander (understandably) took issue with this remark, and hurled his drinking cup at Attalus. Philip, in turn, besotted with love and wine, drew his sword and lunged at his son. But he stumbled and fell amid the couches of the banquet, impaired by drink and an old war injury.

When the groom awoke the next morning to the sobering reality, Alexander was already on his way to Epirus, the ancestral home of his mother, who accompanied him. From there he meant to journey to the kingdom of the Illyrians, the traditional enemy of Macedon, intending to reassert his birthright with their aid. But this right had never really been challenged by Philip, at least not intentionally, and diplomacy served eventually to bring about the son's return and a reconciliation.

The abrasive Attalus had, in the interval, been sent with Parmenion and an army to establish a beachhead in Asia Minor. But there were nevertheless in Macedonia those who resented Attalus and feared the fulfilment of his prayer. Many looked to Philip's nephew, Amyntas son of Perdiccas, who had ruled briefly as a minor, but had been forced to yield the kingship to his uncle. Instead of eliminating him as a potential rival, Philip allowed him to live as a private citizen and married him to one of his

*Cleopatra*

The name Cleopatra is commonly associated with Egypt: virtually everyone is familiar with Cleopatra VII, the mistress of Julius Caesar and Mark Antony, who died in 30 BC. But the name occurs already in Homer's *Iliad* and was popular in ancient Macedonia. Archelaus I's queen, Philip's seventh wife and Alexander the Great's sister were all Cleopatras. It was actually the daughter of the Seleucid king Antiochus III who became the first Cleopatra to rule Egypt, when in 194/3 she married the young king Ptolemy V Epiphanes.

daughters, Cynnane. Now in 337/336 he became the focus of a dissident group, an unwilling candidate for the throne, supported by a faction from Upper Macedonia that planned the assassination of Philip.

This at least was the official version that followed the deed; the version promulgated by Alexander, perhaps with the aim of diverting attention from the true culprits – for

Medallion with the head of Alexander's mother Olympias, from a series of medallions commissioned by the Roman Emperor Caracalla (AD 212–17). This queen, one of Philip's seven wives, had a profound influence on her son's character and also created considerable political mischief in Macedonia during Alexander's absence in Asia. (ISI)

*Philip's marriages*

'In the twenty years of his rule Philip married the Illyrian Audata, by whom he had a daughter, Cynnane, and he also married Phila, sister of Derdas and Machatas. Then, since he wished to extend his realm to include the Thessalian nation, he had children by two Thessalian women, Nicesipolis of Pherae, who bore him Thessalonice, and Philinna of Larissa, by whom he produced Arrhidaeus. In addition, he took possession of the Molossian kingdom by marrying Olympias, by whom he had Alexander and Cleopatra, and when he took Thrace the Thracian king Cothelas came to him with his daughter Meda and many gifts. After marrying Meda, Philip also took her home to be a second wife along with Olympias. In addition to all these wives he also married Cleopatra, with whom he was in love; she was the daughter of Hippostratus and niece of Attalus. By bringing her home as another wife alongside Olympias he made a total shambles of his life. For straightaway, right at the wedding ceremony, Attalus made the remark "Well, now we shall certainly see royalty born who are legitimate and not bastards". Hearing this, Alexander hurled the cup he had in his hands at Attalus, who in turn hurled his goblet at Alexander.

After that Olympias took refuge with the Molossians and Alexander with the Illyrians, and Cleopatra presented Philip with a daughter who was called Europa.' Athenaeus 13.557 (J. C. Yardley trans.)

there were many who held Alexander himself responsible, or, failing that, the jilted queen, his mother. It was an act in keeping with her character, and certainly she voiced no public disapproval, though we may doubt that she crowned the assassin, Pausanias of Orestis, who had been killed as he tried to escape and whose body was subsequently impaled.

*The assassination of Philip II*

'In the meantime, as the auxiliary troops from Greece were assembling, Philip celebrated the marriage of his daughter Cleopatra to that Alexander whom he had made King of Epirus. The day was remarkable for its sumptuous preparations, which befitted the greatness of the two kings, the one giving away a daughter and the other taking a wife. There were also splendid games. Philip was hurrying to see these, flanked by the two Alexanders, his son and his son-in-law, without bodyguards, when Pausanias, a young Macedonian nobleman whom nobody suspected, took up a position in a narrow alleyway and cut Philip down as he went by, thus polluting with funereal sorrow a day set aside for rejoicing ... It is thought that Olympias and her son ... incited Pausanias to proceed to so heinous a crime ... At all events, Olympias had horses ready for the assassin's getaway. Afterwards, when she heard of the King's murder, she came quickly to the funeral, ostensibly doing her duty; and on the night of her arrival she set a golden crown on Pausanias' head while he still hung on the cross, something which no one else but she could have done while Philip's son was still alive. A few days later, she had the murderer's body taken down and cremated it over the remains of her husband; she then erected a tomb for him in the same place and, by inspiring superstition in the people, saw to it that funerary offerings were made to him every year. After this she forced Cleopatra, for whom Philip had divorced her, to hang herself, having first murdered her daughter in the mother's arms, and it was from the sight of her rival hanging there that Olympias gained the vengeance she had accelerated by murder. Finally she consecrated to Apollo the sword with which the King was stabbed, doing so

under the name Myrtale, which was the name that Olympias bore as a little girl. All this was done so openly that she appears to have been afraid that the crime might not be clearly demonstrated as her work.'
Justin 9.6.1–4, 7.8–14 (J. C. Yardley, trans.)

Marble bust believed to be Aristotle. As a boy, Alexander had been educated by Leonidas and Lysimachus, tutors selected by his mother. In 343 BC, Aristotle, whose father Nicomachus had been a physician at the court of Philip's father, Amyntas III, was summoned to Macedonia from Asia Minor and taught Alexander at Mieza. His attitudes towards barbarians (non-Greeks) whom he regarded as inferior and worthy of being slaves of the Greeks, did not rub off on his pupil. (Ann Ronan Picture Library)

Alexander was quick to mete out punishment, freeing himself at the same time of rivals for the throne. Antipater, who had in the past served as regent of Macedon in Philip's absence, supported Alexander's claims, and it was an easy matter to round up and execute rivals on charges of conspiracy. Attalus too was found to have been corresponding with the Athenians – an unlikely scenario – and executed on the new king's orders by his colleague, Parmenion. A bloody purge masqueraded as filial piety, and those who could saved themselves by accommodation with the new king or by flight. Both types would resurface during the campaign, having delayed rather than averted the extreme penalty.

## Alexander, the worthy heir

Philip's abortive expedition thus represented a false start. But Alexander acceded to more than just the throne of Macedon; he also inherited his father's Persian campaign. He was doubtless eager to depart, for we are told that as an adolescent he complained to his father that he was leaving little for him to conquer.

Things did not, however, proceed as planned. The accession of Alexander incited rebellion amongst the subject states and the barbarian kingdoms that bordered on Macedonia. And the new king was forced to prove himself, especially in the south, where the Athenian orator Demosthenes, the implacable enemy of Philip II, was deriding Alexander as a child and a fool.

Resistance to the new king in Thessaly was crushed by speed and daring, as steps (known as 'Alexander's Ladder') cut into the side of Mt Ossa allowed the Macedonians to turn the Thessalians' position. They responded with gestures of contrition and recognised Alexander as *archon* of the Thessalian League, a position previously held by his father. An initial uprising by Thebans, Athenians and Spartans was stifled by Alexander's timely arrival in Greece, where he summoned a meeting of the League of Corinth, the very existence of which was symbolic of Macedonian power. The meeting elected him *hegemon* and Philip's successor as *strategos* ('general') of the Panhellenic crusade.

Bust of Demosthenes. The Athenian orator was a bitter opponent of Macedon and of Philip II in particular. At the time of Alexander's accession he mocked him as 'a child' and compared him with the simpleton, Margites. But Demosthenes soon discovered his mistake. Copy of the original by Polyeuktos produced c. 280 BC, Copenhagen. (Ann Ronan Picture Library)

Sparta, however, refused to join the League or make public recognition of Macedonian suzerainty, for they claimed that they could not follow another, since it was their prerogative to lead. Spartan intransigence was to flare into open rebellion in 331, when Agis III attacked Macedonian troops in the Peloponnese, only to be defeated and killed at Megalopolis. For the time being, however, Alexander was content to ignore them, as they bore their military impotence with ill grace.

Nevertheless, the Greek city-states were not yet ready to renounce all claims to independence and leadership. Alexander clearly thought that he had cowed them into submission with the mere show of force, and

The remains of Pella, birthplace of Alexander the Great. (Greek Ministry of Culture)

he now turned to deal with the border tribes of the Illyrians and Triballians before turning his attentions to Asia. Both were subdued in short order, though in each case the training and discipline of the Macedonian troops made the task seem easier than it was. It was an efficient fighting machine that Philip had left to his son, and Macedonian dominion in the east was built on the foundations of Philip's military reforms.

But Alexander's activities in the north gave rise to rumours – false, but deliberately spread – that the King had been killed in Illyria. In spring 335 the Thebans threw off the Macedonian yoke, besieging the garrison that Philip had planted on their acropolis (the Cadmea) after Chaeronea and claiming

Alexander's response was quick and brutal: within two weeks he was before the gates of Thebes. Athens and Demosthenes proved that they were more capable of inciting others to mischief than of supporting the causes they had so nobly espoused. Through their inaction, they saved themselves and stood by as Alexander dealt most harshly with Thebes, which would now become an example to the other Greek *poleis*: Alexander would tolerate no rebellion in his absence, and he would regard those who preferred the barbarian cause to that of their fellow Greeks as Medisers and traitors to the common cause. Indeed, the city had a long history of Medism, and there was a

to champion the Hellenic cause. The cornerstone of Macedonian propaganda had been the claim that Philip had unified the Greeks for the purpose of attacking Persia, the 'common enemy of Greece', and avenging past wrongs. In this he was merely borrowing the sentiments of Isocrates and other Panhellenists. But the Thebans now proposed to use Persian funds to liberate Greece from the true oppressor, Macedon.

*Panhellenism and anti-Persian sentiment*
    'I maintain that you [Philip] should be the benefactor of Greece, and King of Macedon, and gain to the greatest possible extent the empire of the non-Greek world. If you accomplish this, you will win universal gratitude: from the Greeks for the benefits they gain, from Macedonia if your rule is kingly and not tyrannical, and from the rest of the world if it is through you that they are liberated from Persian despotism and exchange it for Greek protection.'
Isocrates, *Philip* 153 (A. N. W. Saunders trans., Penguin).

*A contrary view*
    'For, personally, I am not in agreement with the Corinthian Demaratus who claimed that the Greeks missed a very pleasurable experience in not seeing Alexander seated on Darius' throne. Actually, I think they might have had more reason to shed tears at the realisation that the men who left this honour to Alexander were those who sacrificed the armies of the Greeks at Leuctra, Coronea, and Corinth and in Arcadia.'
Plutarch, *Agesilaus* 15.3–4 (J. C. Yardley trans.)

Ivory portrait head of Alexander. (Archaeological Museum of Thessaloniki)

tradition that the allied Greeks, at the time of Xerxes' invasion, had sworn the 'Oath of Plataea', which called for the destruction of the city.

Officially, the razing of Thebes could be presented as the initial act of the war of vengeance. (Gryneum in Asia Minor would suffer a similar fate, with the same justification.) Terror would prove more effective than any garrison. To avert the charge of senseless brutality, Alexander portrayed the decision to destroy the city and enslave its population as the work of the Phocians and disaffected Boeotians, for even in those days, inveterate hatred knew no respect for human life.

Persuaded by Demades, the Athenians sent an embassy to congratulate Alexander on his victories in the north and to beg forgiveness for their own recent indiscretions. The King demanded that they surrender the worst trouble-makers, ten prominent orators and generals, including Demosthenes, Lycurgus and Hyperides, but in the event only one, Charidemus, was offered up, and he promptly fled to the court of Darius III.

# Alexander conquers an empire

## Asia Minor

The Macedonian advance forces under Parmenion and Attalus encountered stubborn resistance in Asia Minor after landing there in spring 336. Although they captured Cyzicus, and thus threatened Dascylium, the capital of Hellespontine Phrygia, their push southward was thwarted by Memnon the Rhodian, a son-in-law of the Persian Artabazus and brother of the mercenary captain who had helped Artaxerxes III recapture Egypt in the 340s. Memnon's successes were followed by the arrest and execution of Attalus, which probably did nothing to raise the morale of the army. Parmenion did, however, take Gryneum, sacking the town and enslaving its inhabitants, for the city had a history of 'Medism'. Elsewhere, another colleague of Parmenion, Callas son of Harpalus, who had perhaps come out as Attalus's replacement, was confined to the coastline. All in all, the expeditionary force had not made a good beginning.

The advent of Alexander, with an army of about 40,000, altered the situation dramatically. The satraps of Asia Minor led their territorial levies into Hellespontine Phrygia and held a council of war at Zeleia. Here they rejected Memnon's proposal that they adopt a 'scorched earth' policy, opting instead to challenge the Macedonian army at the nearby Granicus river.

Asia Minor was no stranger to Greek invasion. In the 390s, Tissaphernes and Pharnabazus, the satraps of Sardis and Dascylium, proved adequate to deal with forces dispatched by Sparta and, in fact, played each other false for the sake of minor gains. The Macedonian invasion was on a different scale, with much greater avowed intentions, for the Persians were not ignorant of the creation of the League of Corinth, or of its mandate to wage war against them. Some sources, and possibly Alexander himself (for official purposes), charged the Persian King with trying to pre-empt the expedition by engineering Philip's assassination. If there was any truth to the charge, the act itself had little effect. Indeed, it replaced a more cautious commander with a daring and ambitious one. The reality of Alexander's presence on Asian soil demanded immediate and concerted action.

The Persians continued to hire large numbers of Greek mercenaries, who for once were fighting for more than pay. Like many

*The composition of Alexander's army*
'It was found that, of infantry, there were 12,000 Macedonians, 7,000 allies and 5,000 mercenaries. These were all under the command of Parmenion. The Odrysians, Triballians and Illyrians accompanying him numbered 7,000, and there were a thousand archers and so-called Agrianes, so that the infantry totalled 32,000. Cavalry numbers were as follows: 1,800 Macedonians, commanded by Parmenion's son Philotas; 1,800 Thessalians, commanded by Callas, the son of Harpalus; from the rest of Greece a total of 600, commanded by Erigyius; and 900 Thracian guides and Paeonians, with Cassander as their commander. This made a total of 4,500 cavalry.

Such was the strength of the army that crossed to Asia with Alexander. The number of soldiers left behind in Europe, who were under Antipater's command, totalled 12,000 infantry and 15,000 cavalry.'
Diodorus 17.17.3–5 (J. C. Yardley trans.)

of their compatriots at home, they doubtless regarded Persia as the lesser evil, and Alexander for his part treated captured mercenaries harshly, as traitors rather than defeated enemies. The Persian commanders, however, failed to appreciate the personal motivations of the Greek mercenaries and their leaders: distrustful of the very men who had nothing to gain by surrendering, they viewed Memnon with suspicion and negated the effectiveness of the mercenary infantry. At any rate, they stationed their cavalry on the eastern bank of the Granicus river and kept the Greek infantry in reserve. Before these saw action, the battle had been lost.

The Persian cavalry proved to be no match, in tactics or hand-to-hand combat, for the European horsemen. Two would-be champions were felled by Alexander's *sarissa*, a third was in the act of striking the King

when slain. Most of the prominent Persian leaders were among the dead; Arsites escaped the battlefield, only to die by his own hand; Arsames fled to Cilicia, to fight again at Issus.

Upon receiving the news of the Persian disaster at the Granicus, Mithrenes, the commandant of Sardis, chose to surrender to Alexander despite the city's strong natural defences. His judgement proved sound, for Alexander kept him in his entourage and treated him with respect, eventually entrusting him with the governorship of Armenia. But the Greek cities of the coast continued to resist, in part because history had taught them that the Persian yoke was lighter than that of previous 'liberators', but also because Memnon's army and the Persian fleet limited their options.

The cities of Miletus and Halicarnassus both offered fierce resistance. The former

### Alexander at the Granicus

'Alexander plunged into the river with 13 cavalry squadrons. He was now driving into enemy projectiles towards an area that was sheer and protected by armed men and cavalry, and negotiating a current that swept his men off their feet and pulled them under. His leadership seemed madcap and senseless rather than prudent. Even so, he persisted with the crossing and, after great effort and hardship, made it to the targeted area, which was wet and slippery with mud. He was immediately forced into a disorganised battle and to engage, man against man, the enemies who came bearing down on them, before the troops making the crossing could get into some sort of formation.

The Persians came charging at these with a shout. They lined up their horses against those of their enemy and fought with their lances and then, when the lances were shattered, with their swords. A large number closed in on the King, who stood out because of his shield and the crest on his helmet, on each side of

which there was plume striking for its whiteness and its size. Alexander received a spear in the joint of his cuirass, but was not wounded. Then the Persian generals Rhoesaces and Spithridates came at him together. Sidestepping the latter, Alexander managed to strike Rhoesaces, who was wearing a cuirass, with his spear, but when he shattered this he resorted to his sword. While the two were engaged hand-to-hand, Spithridates brought his horse to a halt beside them and, swiftly pulling himself up from the animal, dealt the King a blow with the barbarian battle-axe. He broke off Alexander's crest, along with one of the plumes, and the helmet only just held out against the blow, the blade of the axe actually touching the top of the King's hair. Spithridates then began to raise the axe for a second blow but Cleitus (the Black) got there first, running him through with his spear. At the same moment Rhosaeces also fell, struck down by a sword-blow from Alexander.
Plutarch, *Alexander* 16.3–11 (J. C. Yardley trans.)

could count on support from the Persian fleet until the occupation of Mycale by Philotas deprived it of a base. At Halicarnassus, daring sallies were made against Alexander's siege equipment, but eventually the city was betrayed by the commanders of the army, Orontopates and Memnon, who abandoned it to the Macedonians. Alexander restored to the throne Ada, the widow of the previous ruler, who had been supplanted by Orontopates, and allowed her to become his adoptive mother – in effect, reserving for himself the hereditary claim to Caria. (Philip had taught his son that not all power was gained by the sword.) By winter 334/333, Alexander had made considerable headway in the conquest of Asia Minor, but he had yet to face Darius III and the weight of the Persian army.

For Darius, the necessity of taking the field in person was less than welcome, since the Great King had had only a brief respite from the chaos that attended his accession. In spite of the débâcle at the Granicus, the Persian situation was far from critical: a counter-offensive in the Aegean was beginning to enjoy some success, with the anti-Macedonian forces regaining ground on Lesbos and at Halicarnassus. But Memnon died suddenly from illness. To replace him Darius appointed Pharnabazus, who assigned the naval command to Datames and met with the Spartan King, Agis, near Siphnos in the hope of encouraging an uprising in the Peloponnese.

At Gordium Alexander had fulfilled – or, perhaps, cheated – the prophecy that gave dominion over Asia to anyone who could undo the Gordian knot. Frustrated by the intricacies of the knot, he cut it with his sword. Some of the Macedonians were far from convinced that a venture deeper into the heart of the empire would be successful: Harpalus, his personal friend and treasurer, fled shortly before the battle of Issus. The official story was that he had been up to some mischief with a scoundrel named Tauriscus, but Harpalus may have had serious misgivings about his king's chances. To complicate matters further, Alexander had

## Harpalus, the Imperial Treasurer

Harpalus, son of Machatas, belonged to one of the royal houses of Upper Macedonia, that of Elimea. Afflicted by a physical ailment that left him unfit for military service, he nevertheless served Alexander in other ways. In the 330s he served as one of Alexander's *hetairoi*, in this case, probably one of the Crown Prince's advisers; he was exiled by Philip for encouraging Alexander to offer himself as a prospective husband of the Carian princess Ada, whom Philip had planned to marry off to his half-witted son, Arrhidaeus. Harpalus was appointed treasurer early in the campaign, but he became involved with an unscrupulous individual named Tauriscus, who persuaded him to flee from Alexander's camp – no doubt he absconded with a sum of the King's money. Alexander, however, forgave and recalled him, reinstating him as treasurer.

Later in the campaign, when the King had gone to India and Harpalus remained in Babylon, the latter enjoyed a life of extravagance and debauchery, importing delicacies for his table and courtesans for his bed. When news arrived that Alexander was returning from the east, he fled to Athens, taking with him vast sums of money, and attempted to induce the Athenians to go to war. Rebuffed by the Athenians – at least, on an official level – he sailed away to Crete, where he was murdered by one of his followers, a certain Pausanias.

been struck down by fever – probably a bout of malaria – after bathing in the Cydnus river, and it was not at all certain that he would survive.

Darius, for his part, had attracted to his cause the largest force of Greek mercenaries employed by a Persian king in the history of Achaemenid rule – 30,000 Greeks, according to the official historian, Callisthenes. Amongst these was Amyntas, son of

Antiochus, who had been a supporter of Alexander's cousin and rival, Amyntas IV, and who fled Macedonia soon after Philip's assassination. Another leader of mercenaries was Charidemus, a longstanding enemy of Macedon. Charidemus, as it turned out, fell victim to court intrigue, but Amyntas gave a good account of himself before escaping from the battlefield with some 4,000 mercenaries, only to find adventure and death in Egypt.

Darius's army, which the Alexander historians (Curtius, Justin, Diodorus and Arrian) estimated at between 312,000 and 600,000, moved from Babylon to Sochi, where it encamped at the beginning of autumn 333. Alexander, meanwhile, reached the coastal plain of Cilicia and the Pillar of Jonah – the so-called 'Syrian' or 'Assyrian' Gates – south of modern Iskenderun, which gave access to Syria. In fact, it was in order to avoid the Belen Pass that the Persians entered Cilicia via the Amanic Gates (the Bahçe Pass) and reached Issus through Toprakkale. To Alexander's surprise, the positions of the two armies were now reversed, with Darius situated north of the Pinarus river and astride the Macedonian lines of communication. By the same token, there was nothing to prevent Alexander from marching into Syria except the danger to his rear.

But if the protagonists were to meet, it was advantageous for Alexander to fight in the restricted terrain of Cilicia, where the mountains and sea reduced the mobility of the enemy's troops and negated his numerical superiority. Even Alexander, who seized the narrows to the south on the night before the engagement, had to march his smaller army considerably forward into the widening coastal plain before he could deploy his infantry in a line and leave sufficient room for the cavalry to protect the flanks. He positioned himself with the Companion Cavalry on the right wing, hard against the hills that restricted movement.

Darius sent a force south of the Pinarus in order to buy time for the deployment of his own troops. Now that it was clear that the

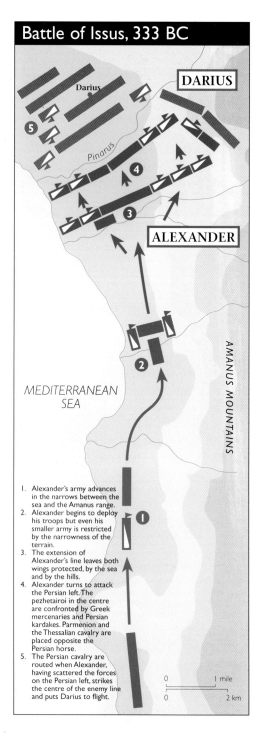

**Battle of Issus, 333 BC**

Darius

DARIUS

Pinarus

ALEXANDER

MEDITERRANEAN SEA

AMANUS MOUNTAINS

1. Alexander's army advances in the narrows between the sea and the Amanus range.
2. Alexander begins to deploy his troops but even his smaller army is restricted by the narrowness of the terrain.
3. The extension of Alexander's line leaves both wings protected, by the sea and by the hills.
4. Alexander turns to attack the Persian left. The pezhetairoi in the centre are confronted by Greek mercenaries and Persian kardakes. Parmenion and the Thessalian cavalry are placed opposite the Persian horse.
5. The Persian cavalry are routed when Alexander, having scattered the forces on the Persian left, strikes the centre of the enemy line and puts Darius to flight.

0        1 mile
0            2 km

Macedonians would not be overawed by Persian numbers, he took a defensive position, using the banks of the Pinarus as

Relief of Persian guards from Persepolis. (TRIP)

an added impediment; where the riverbanks gave insufficient protection, he erected palisades. A bid to move forces behind the Macedonian position, in the hills, proved ineffective, and Alexander drove them to seek refuge in higher ground by using the Agrianes and the archers; in the event, they were not a factor in the battle of Issus.

That Alexander, in imitation of the younger Cyrus at Cunaxa, charged directly at the Persian centre, where Darius himself was positioned, may be more than mere fiction. There was something in the mentality of the age that required leaders to seek each other out. (One is reminded of Alexander's apocryphal remark that he would participate in the Olympic games but only if he competed with princes!) But, if the story is true, this must have occurred in the second phase of the battle, when Alexander turned to deal with the Greek infantry that were exploiting a breach in the Macedonian phalanx.

The Greek infantry occupied the centre of the line and were most encumbered by the terrain. While Alexander routed the Persian left, which shattered on the initial assault, the heavy infantry in the centre surged forward, losing its cohesiveness. (The pattern would repeat itself at Gaugamela, with more dangerous results.) Here, opposite them, Darius had stationed his 30,000 Greek infantry, supported by 60,000 picked infantrymen whom the Persians called

Kardakes, half on each side. Against these troops the vaunted Macedonian *pezhetairoi* found it difficult to advance, and here they suffered the majority of their casualties, including the taxiarch Ptolemy, son of Seleucus.

Having put the Persian left to flight, Alexander now wheeled to his own left, slamming into the Greek mercenaries and destroying their formation. Before he could come to grips with the Great King, the Persian ranks broke and Darius fled in his chariot. Hampered in his flight by the rough terrain, he abandoned his chariot and mounted a horse to make good his escape; as an added precaution he removed his royal insignia and eluded the enemy under the cover of darkness.

Some 100,000 Persian infantry were either killed or captured at Issus, along with 10,000 horsemen, for the armoured horse, which had fought gallantly, dispersed when it learned of Darius's flight, only to suffer more grievously in their bid for safety. Among the captives were found the mother,

Detail from the Alexander Mosaic at Pompeii. Darius III prepares to flee the battlefield. (Ann Ronan Picture Library)

---

*Alexander's alleged encounter with Darius*
'In this action he received a sword wound in the thigh: according to Chares this was given him by Darius, with whom he engaged in hand-to-hand combat. Alexander sent a letter to Antipater describing the battle, but made no mention in it of who had given him the wound: he said no more than that he had been stabbed in the thigh with a dagger and that the wound was not a dangerous one.'
Plutarch, *Alexander* 20 (I. Scott-Kilvert trans., Penguin)

The Alexander Mosaic. Darius and the Persians under attack by Alexander. (Ann Ronan Picture Library)

wife and children of Darius himself. By contrast, Alexander's losses were slight. But we have only Macedonian propaganda to go by, and figures, like the sensational stories of Alexander struggling with Darius in person, must be treated with caution.

After the staggering defeat at Issus, Damascus fell into the hands of Parmenion. The amount of treasure and the importance of the individuals captured there reveal that the city was not merely a convenient place to deposit the treasures and non-combatants, but that Darius had intended to move his base of operations forward. He clearly did not expect to be routed in a single

*Antigonus the One-Eyed*

An officer of Philip II's generation, Antigonus was already approaching 60 when he accompanied Alexander to Asia. In the spring of 333 he was left behind as the governor (*satrap*) of Phrygia, which had its administrative centre at Celaenae. There he remained for the duration of the war, attended by his wife Stratonice and his sons, one of whom, Demetrius, was to become the famous *Poliorcetes* ('the Besieger'). After Alexander's death, Antigonus emerged as one of the leading Successors and, together with his son, made a bid for supreme power. He died, however, on the battlefield of Ipsus in 301, and Demetrius, who experienced his share of victories and defeats, proved to possess more showmanship than generalship. But ultimately his son, named after his paternal grandfather, was to establish the Antigonid dynasty in Macedonia.

Detail of Alexander from the Alexander Mosaic, now at Pompeii. Alexander is intent upon attacking Darius in person. (Ann Ronan Picture Library)

Sisygambis, mother of Darius III, mistakes Hephaestion for
Alexander the Great after the Persian defeat at Issus in
333 BC. Painting by Francisco de Mura (1696–1782).
(Ann Ronan Picture Library)

engagement and forced to seek refuge in the
centre of the empire.

For Alexander the victory – particularly in
the aftermath of Memnon's death – provided
the opportunity of pushing ahead himself with
the conquest and leaving his newly appointed
satraps to deal with the continued resistance in
Asia Minor. Antigonus the One-Eyed, a certain
Ptolemy (perhaps even a kinsman of
Antigonus) and Balacrus dealt effectively with
what Persian forces remained behind.

## Phoenicia and Egypt

In Phoenicia, meanwhile, the news of Issus led
to defection on a large scale. Representatives of

the coastal cities brought Alexander crowns of gold that symbolised their surrender: Aradus, Marathus and Byblus submitted in short order. And, although the cities themselves received good treatment from the conqueror, there were some rulers, like Straton (Abd-astart) of Sidon, who despite their surrender were deposed. It appears that the Sidonians, who now welcomed Alexander as a 'liberator' – for Artaxerxes III had put down an insurrection in the city with the utmost brutality – were not inclined to retain in power a man with a lengthy record of collaboration with the Persians. According to the tradition, Alexander allowed his best friend, Hephaestion, to select a new king: he found a scion of the royal house, Abdalonymus, reduced by poverty to working as a gardener, and upon him he bestowed the crown.

The capture of Phoenicia added a new dimension to Alexander's campaign, one that must not be downplayed. The area was critical for the survival of the Persian fleet, which was, in turn, Darius's chief hope of defeating Alexander if he could not do so on the battlefields of the east. Alexander had abandoned all attempts at defeating the Persian navy at sea and had disbanded the Macedonian fleet: it was numerically inferior, just as its ships and sailors were of inferior quality; and, to make matters worse, the Greek naval powers, especially the Athenians, could not be fully trusted. It was better to deprive the Persian navy of its bases and thereby reduce its power, without running the risk of a military disaster at sea that might turn the tide of the war but would almost certainly tarnish Alexander's reputation as an invincible foe.

Alexander's naval strategy worked. As the inhabitants and governments of each region surrendered to him, their naval contingents too abandoned the Persian cause. The Phoenicians found themselves in an awkward position, since large numbers of their citizens, including many of their local dynasts, served with the Persian fleet. These rulers especially found it preferable to surrender to Alexander in the hope of retaining their power rather than remain

*Hephaestion, Alexander's alter ego*

Hephaestion, son of Amyntor, had been a close friend of the King since boyhood. He had been with Alexander as a teenager at Mieza, when the Crown Prince was educated by Aristotle. Romanticised accounts compared the two with Achilles and Patroclus. Whether they were lovers, as many modern writers like to assert, is not entirely clear. But Alexander certainly promoted Hephaestion's career despite the fact that he seems to have possessed poor leadership qualities and little military skill. He was nevertheless a gifted organiser and Alexander left many matters of logistics – supply, transport of equipment, bridge-building and the founding of settlements – to him.

By the time the army reached India, Hephaestion's promotion had brought about friction with other officers, especially the fine soldier Craterus. At one point the two came to blows in front of their respective troops and Alexander had to intervene. Although he chided Hephaestion because he failed to recognise that 'without Alexander he would be nothing', he remained devoted to his lifelong friend. In October 324, Hephaestion died of illness, and the King was inconsolable.

loyal to Darius. By contrast, the inland Syrians were more inclined to stay with Darius, and we find them joining their former satrap, Mazaeus, in the army that faced Alexander again in 331 at Gaugamela.

Darius meanwhile resorted to diplomacy, for his family had fallen into the victor's hands when the Persian camp was taken after the King's flight from Issus. Letters were sent to Alexander offering money and territory in exchange for Darius's kinfolk. But the exchanges between the two kings demonstrated merely the Persian King's refusal to recognise the gravity of the danger to the empire. Furthermore, Darius persisted

ΓΝΛΕΙΣΕΓΟΗΣΕΝ

Relief showing a hunting scene. Hephaestion is the figure with the raised sword. He was Alexander's boyhood friend and alter ego. In 324 BC he married the younger daughter of Darius III, and thus became the brother-in-law of one of Alexander's own Persian brides, the princess Stateira. In October of the same year he died of an illness at Ecbatana. (Greek Ministry of Culture)

in treating Alexander as an upstart, an inferior who could, as he thought, be bought off with the cession of Asia Minor and 10,000 talents.

But Alexander held the trump cards and was not prepared to fold, when diplomacy offered less than he had obtained by conquest. Negotiations continued for almost two years, with an escalation of the terms – Darius was eventually to offer Asia west of the Euphrates, 30,000 talents and the hand of his daughter in marriage – but Persian concessions failed to keep pace with Macedonian conquests. Darius no longer had the authority to dispose of Alexander's 'spear-won land'.

Whereas the northern Phoenician cities had capitulated on the news of Alexander's approach, Tyre resisted the King's request to make sacrifices to Hercules (Melqart) within their city. This was, of course, a transparent ploy to gain control of the place. But the Tyrians could afford to be defiant, or at least so they thought, for about half a mile (0.8km) of sea separated them from the Macedonian army, and the city fathers responded that Alexander was welcome to

A modern Greek coin depicting Alexander wearing the diadem and the Horns of Amun, the Egyptian deity whom the Greeks regarded as a ram-headed Zeus. The inscription on top reads 'megas Alexandros' (Alexander the Great). On his own coinage and in his own time this epithet was never used. (TRIP)

sacrifice to Hercules at 'Old Tyre', which was situated on the mainland. Furthermore, there was the expectation – vain, as it turned out – of aid from their North African colony, Carthage. Neither grand strategy nor Alexander's reputation, however, could allow the young king to bypass the city.

Alexander realised that the siege of an island city would be no easy matter, and that a lengthy siege would buy valuable time for his enemy. Hence, he sent heralds into the city in the hope of persuading the Tyrians to surrender. But the diplomatic approaches were rebuffed, and the heralds executed and thrown into the sea. Work began immediately upon the building of a causeway from the mainland to the island.

In the early stages the work went well and quickly, because the water was shallower near the mainland and out of range of Tyrian missiles. As the mole approached the city, however, ships began to harass the workers, and Alexander erected two towers, with hides and canvases to shield the workers and with turrets from which to shower missiles upon the enemy. To this the Tyrians responded by sending a fire-ship against the end of the mole, driving off the

Macedonians and burning their towers to the ground. Here the ancient sources diverge on the matter of the causeway, and it is not certain whether Alexander began a new one, approaching the city from a different angle, or merely widened the existing one. In the event, the mole did not prove to be the decisive factor, since the city walls, which rose 160ft (50m) above the point of attack, were most heavily fortified at that very point and could not be shaken by battering rams.

Instead the critical support came from the Cypriotes and Phoenicians, many of whom had abandoned the Persian fleet of Autophradates once they received news that their cities had surrendered. These ships gave Alexander the advantage on the sea and the Tyrians were content to block their harbour entrances – when they did sail out, it was with heavy losses. Using the fleet to assail the walls, Alexander found that the south side of the city had the weakest

### The importance of Tyre

'Friends and fellow soldiers, I do not see how we can safely advance upon Egypt, so long as Persia controls the sea; and to pursue Darius with the neutral city of Tyre in our rear and Egypt and Cyprus still in enemy hands would be a serious risk, especially in view of the situation in Greece. With our army on the track of Darius, far inland in the direction of Babylon, the Persians might well regain control of the coast, and thus be enabled with more power behind them to transfer the war to Greece, where Sparta is already openly hostile to us, and Athens, at the moment, is but an unwilling ally; fear, not friendliness, keeping her on our side. But with Tyre destroyed, all Phoenicia would be ours, and the Phoenician fleet, which both in numbers and quality is the predominant element in the sea-power of Persia, would very like come over to us.'
Arrian 2.18 (A. de Sélincourt trans., Penguin)

The Libyan oasis of Siwah, where Alexander was acknowledged by the priests as the 'Son of Amun', hence legitimate pharaoh of Egypt. (TRIP)

fortifications, and these he assaulted until a breach occurred. Once the walls had given way, the defenders were virtually helpless, but they fought desperately. The citizens paid for their defiance in the slaughter that ensued, though many Sidonians helped to save their fellow Phoenicians from the enemy's rage.

Gaza, too, resisted Alexander, but the city fell after only two months. By contrast, Egypt, which now lay open, welcomed the Macedonians as liberators. Thus ended the last period of Persian occupation and the brief reign of the Thirty-First Dynasty. Alexander's legitimacy as Egyptian pharaoh was proclaimed in Memphis and given divine sanction at the Libyan oasis of Siwah, where the conqueror was greeted as the 'son of Amun'.

## Uprising in Greece

When Alexander returned to Tyre, after his lengthy sojourn in Egypt, he learned of serious unrest in the Peloponnese. There the Spartan King, Agis III, who had begun his dealings with the Persian leaders in the Aegean very soon after Alexander's departure from Europe, openly resisted Macedonian power. In a bold move he defeated the army of Corrhagus, thus forcing Antipater himself to lead an army to the south. Nor was Agis's force inconsequential: he had collected 22,000 men from the neighbouring states of Elis, Arcadia and Achaea, and with these he now laid siege to Megalopolis. (This was the city that the Theban general Epaminondas had founded when he invaded the Peloponnese and ended Sparta's hegemony there.)

Antipater was, however, preoccupied with affairs in Thrace, where the *strategos* (military governor) of the region, Memnon, was in open rebellion. This was clearly not done by prearrangement with Agis and the anti-Macedonian forces in the south, for Memnon quickly came to terms with Antipater and thus freed him to deal with the Greek insurrection. Furthermore, the fact that Memnon later brought reinforcements to Alexander in the east suggests that the King did not regard his actions as treasonous.

The Macedonian army confronted Agis at Megalopolis in the summer of 331 – certainly the entire rebellion had been suppressed before the battle of Gaugamela was fought. The contest was a renewal of the bitter struggle between Macedon and the Greeks, who had still not accepted the suzerainty of the former. Although he fell on

*Alexander makes light of Antipater's victory over Agis III at Megalopolis*
'Alexander even added a joke when he was told of the war waged by Antipater against Agis. "Men," he said, "it appears that while we were in the process of vanquishing Darius, there was a battle of mice over there in Arcadia.'
Plutarch, *Life of Agesilaus* 15 (J. C. Yardley trans.)

the battlefield, Agis did not sell his life cheaply; nor did the 5,300 other Greeks who perished in the battle. Alexander, when he learned of the engagement, dismissed it as insignificant. But the contest had left 3,500 Macedonians dead, and until it had been decided his activities in the east were suspended in uncertainty.

## The final clash with Darius

While Alexander directed his attentions to Phoenicia and Egypt, Darius, once his attempts to win a negotiated settlement had failed, marshalled another army. If there was anything that the empire had in abundance, it was manpower; though, as Darius would learn, mere numbers of men would not suffice against a brilliant tactician like Alexander. Nevertheless, the barbarian army at Gaugamela contained several contingents that had faced the Macedonians before. Syrians, defeated at Issus but steadfast in their loyalty to Persia, stood shoulder to shoulder with Persians, Babylonians and Medes, who formed the nucleus of the Great King's strength.

Nevertheless, the composition of Darius's army was radically different from that which had been routed at Issus, for it included the fine horsemen from the Upper Satrapies (Central Asia) – not just the Arians, Arachosians and Bactrians, but the Scythian cavalry of the Dahae, Sacae and Massagetae – which Darius had either been unable to mobilise or considered superfluous in 333.

Not restricted by the terrain as they had been at Issus, the Persians were more confident of victory on the expansive plains of northern Mesopotamia. And here too they would bring to bear the terrifying spectacle of scythed chariots and elephants.

As he had done at Issus, Darius prepared the battlefield, which was littered with obstacles and traps for the unsuspecting enemy, though these were revealed by deserters and their effectiveness negated. But primarily the Persians relied on vastly superior numbers and the luxury of deploying them as they chose on the plains beyond the Tigris. Darius expected to outflank and envelop the Macedonian army, which was pitifully small by comparison. The scythed chariots, making a frontal charge, proved ineffectual: Alexander's javelin-men simply parted ranks upon their approach and shot down their drivers or their teams. The chariot had become a symbol of oriental vanity, for its effectiveness had already been challenged by infantrymen at the end of the Bronze Age, and it remained a splendid anachronism, but no match for cool minds and brave hearts.

Some aspects of the battle of Gaugamela are reminiscent of Issus – not surprisingly, since Alexander's method was to drive hard at the Persian left while the infantry held the centre. This time, however, his infantry did not attack the centre head-on, as the Macedonians had tackled the Greeks and Kardakes in the first engagement. Instead it advanced obliquely, the hypaspists following closely the cavalry attack, and the remainder of the *pezhetairoi* surging to keep up with the hypaspists. And, just as had happened at Issus, a gap occurred as the phalanx rushed forward, which was again exploited by the enemy. This time, however, Alexander did not turn immediately to aid the phalanx, but instead rode on in pursuit of the Persian left. His thinking was surely that he did not want Darius to escape him a second time.

Nor was the infantry challenged by troops of similar quality to those at Issus. Rather it was the Scythian and Indian cavalry that broke through the line, only to turn their attention to plundering the Macedonian baggage camp. More disciplined were the horsemen stationed on the Persian right. Here Mazaeus's squadrons were exerting pressure on the Macedonian left, under the command of Parmenion. Although the old general eventually overcame his opponents, he had been forced to send riders to

Excavated ruins of Babylon. (TRIP)

summon Alexander to return. It was the proper thing to do, but it was also to harm his reputation, for the official history questioned Parmenion's competence and blamed him for spoiling an otherwise total victory. In truth, it was the steadfastness of Parmenion and Craterus on the left, combined with the rapacity of the barbarian allied horse – who stopped to plunder instead of coming to Mazaeus's aid – that secured the victory at Gaugamela.

Although Darius had again escaped from the battlefield, Gaugamela proved fatal for the Persian Empire. The Great King fled in the direction of Arbela, which he reached by midnight. Other contingents dispersed to their territories, as was the custom amongst the barbarians. Those who commanded the garrisons and guarded the treasures in the empire's capitals made formal surrender to Alexander. One man, Mazaeus, the Persian hero of Gaugamela, surrendered Babylon, together with the *gazophylax* ('guardian of the treasures'), Bagophanes. Alexander entered in great ceremony the ancient city, which now publicly turned its resources over to the new king, as it were.

What the Alexander historians depict as a spontaneous welcome was in fact ritual surrender, enacted so many times in the

past – in ceremony for the legitimate heir to the throne, as well as in earnest for a conquering king. In return, Alexander appointed Mazaeus satrap of Babylon, though he installed a garrison in the city and military overseers (*strategoi*) to ensure the loyalty of the new governor and the population.

Despite Gaugamela's ranking as one of the 'decisive' battles of world history, the fact is that it was only decisive for the Persian side. For Darius it was, one might say, the final nail in the coffin; Alexander, on the other hand, could have survived defeat in northern Mesopotamia and still held the

*Babylon surrenders to the Macedonian conqueror*

'A large number of the Babylonians had taken up a position on the walls, eager to have a view of their new king, but most went out to meet him, including the man in charge of the citadel and royal treasury, Bagophanes. Not to be outdone by Mazaeus in paying his respects to Alexander, Bagophanes had carpeted the whole road with flowers and garlands and set up at intervals on both sides silver altars heaped not just with frankincense but with all manner of perfumes. Following him were his gifts – herds of cattle and horses, and lions, too, and leopards, carried along in cages. Next came the Magi chanting a song in their native fashion, and behind them were the Chaldaeans, then the Babylonians, represented not only by priests but also by musicians equipped with their national instrument. (The role of the latter was to sing the praises of the Persian kings, that of the Chaldaeans to reveal astronomical movements and regular seasonal changes.) At the rear came the Babylonian cavalry, their equipment and that of their horses suggesting extravagance rather than majesty.

Surrounded by an armed guard, the king instructed the townspeople to follow at the rear of his infantry; then he entered the city on a chariot and went to the palace.'
Curtius Rufus, *The History of Alexander* 5.1.19–23 (J. C. Yardley trans., Penguin)

western portion of the empire. Victory, however, belonged to the Macedonians, and the might of Persia was shattered. Babylon had no hope of resisting, and Susa, too, avoided pillage by embracing the conqueror.

The entry of Alexander the Great into Babylon. Painting by Johann Georg Platzer (1704–61). (Ann Ronan Picture Library)

Reconstruction of the Ishtar Gate of Nebuchadrezzar.
(AKG Berlin)

Again the defecting satrap, Aboulites, was
retained and once more a Macedonian
garrison was imposed.

The blueprint had been established:
Alexander would regularly combine a show
of native rule with the fetters of military
occupation. But, with Darius still at large,
Alexander introduced military reforms to
strengthen the army and the command

structures. Reinforcements continued to
arrive, even though the avenging army
moved ever closer to its ultimate goal, that
most hated of all cities: Persepolis.

The satrap of Persis, Ariobarzanes,
had mustered a sizeable force: with
25,000 defenders he blocked the so-called
'Persian' or 'Susidan' Gates in an attempt to
stall the Macedonians until the city's
treasures could be removed. If this was not
his aim, it was certainly Alexander's fear.
Dividing his force in two, Alexander led the

Reconstruction of Babylon showing the Ishtar Gate. (TRIP)

more mobile contingents through the mountains to the rear of the pass, leaving Craterus to fix the enemy's attention on what he perceived as the stalled army. In fact, Ariobarzanes was delaying only a portion of the Macedonian force: the slowest

elements and the baggage-train were following the wagon road into Persis under the command of Parmenion. The satrap's position was circumvented by Alexander, whose men braved the perils of terrain and winter snow, led by captive guides. Ariobarzanes' troops were slaughtered in the pass and it was now a relatively simple matter to bridge the Araxes, whereupon Tiridates surrendered both city and treasure to the Macedonians.

Its symbolic importance – the very meaning of the Greek form of the name Persepolis, 'City of the Persians', enhanced its actual associations with Xerxes and the great invasion – dictated its fate: pillage, rape and massacre ensued. The palace too fell victim to the victor's wrath, but only after the treasures had been removed and shipped to Ecbatana. Then, whether by design or through a spontaneous urge for revenge, it was put to the torch. One version attributed

the burning to an Athenian courtesan, Thaïs, who was to become the mistress of Ptolemy, the later King of Egypt.

The destruction of Persepolis was symbolic rather than total, for it continued as the capital of the province during the age of the Successors. It did, however, illuminate the difficulties faced by the conqueror. For one thing, it could be taken to signify the completion of the war of vengeance, the attainment of the stated goal of the

Battle of Gaugamela, 331 BC, commonly but inaccurately referred to as the battle of Arbela. The town of Arbela was actually some distance from the battlefield, and Darius in his flight did not reach it until after midnight. From the studio of Charles Le Brun (1619–90). (AKG Berlin)

expedition, and the allied troops would naturally assume that it warranted their demobilisation. Still, Alexander could remind them that as long as Darius lived, the mission had not been completed.

Conversely, the destruction of the palace and the maltreatment of the citizens undermined Alexander's propaganda, which had at an early stage sought to portray him as the legitimate successor of the Great King.

Ruins of Persepolis. The palace was put to the torch by Alexander, as an act of policy since the city symbolised past atrocities by Persians against Greeks, but most of the city remained untouched and continued to function during the Hellenistic period. (TRIP)

Rightly had Parmenion advised against such action, reminding Alexander that he should not destroy what was now his own property. Nevertheless, what may have caused resentment in Persia could well have been received with a degree of satisfaction in Babylon and Susa, even Ecbatana, all of which had been overshadowed by the advent of the Achaemenids and the establishment of Persepolis.

Columns of the ancient audience hall at Persepolis. (TRIP)

Persian helmet from Olympia in Greece. (AKG Berlin)

## Advance into Central Asia

At the beginning of 330, Darius retained only one of the four capitals of the empire, Ecbatana (modern Hamadan). It was a convenient location, from which he could receive reports of Alexander's activities in Persia and at the same time summon reinforcements from the Upper Satrapies. Furthermore, it lay astride the Silk Road, the great east–west corridor that ran south of the Elburz mountains and the Caspian and north of the Great Salt Desert. Unfortunately, many of the King's paladins advised against awaiting Alexander in that place, and they urged Darius to withdraw in the direction of Bactria, which lay beyond the Merv oasis, just north-west of modern Afghanistan.

This plan was adopted by Darius, but only when it was too late to elude Alexander, who resumed hostilities once the mountain passes were free of snow. The Great King's column was much too cumbersome: the royal equipment that offered the necessary comforts, and the covered wagons that sheltered the concubines on the journey, made slow progress through the Sar-i-Darreh or Caspian Gates, even though they had been sent in advance of the army. Only 40,000 native troops and 4,000 Greeks remained with Darius, and deserters – many of them prominent men – drifted back towards the Macedonian force that was, every day, shortening the distance between the two armies.

In the remote village of Thara, the chiliarch, Nabarzanes, and Bessus, one of the King's kinsmen, challenged Darius's leadership. Aided by other prominent

Alexander comes upon the dead Persian King. (ISI)

figures, they arrested the King, only to murder him soon afterwards. His body was left by the side of the road in the hope that when Alexander encountered it he might break off the pursuit. Nabarzanes himself attempted to rally support in Hyrcania and Parthia; Bessus continued towards Bactria and Sogdiana, accompanied by 600 horsemen. With Darius dead, he himself assumed the upright tiara, the sign of kingship, and styled himself Artaxerxes, the fifth of that name.

For Alexander, the time had come to call a halt. He had covered some 450 miles (720km) in three weeks: with a larger force he had pushed east from Ecbatana to Rhagae (that is, from Hamadan to Rey, on the edge of modern Teheran), a march of roughly

250 miles (400km), in 11 days; after a five-day rest, he had taken a much smaller, mounted force another 200 miles (320km), coming upon Darius's body late on the sixth day of pursuit. Bessus himself had, for the present, eluded him, but the Macedonian army had scattered in the chase and the daily arrival of high-ranking Persian deserters made it necessary to take stock before turning to deal with the usurper.

Some Persians were installed as satraps – Phrataphernes in Parthia, Autophradates amongst the Tapurians – while others remained in the King's entourage, awaiting suitable employment and reward. Two dangerous men were pardoned, Nabarzanes and Satibarzanes. The former ought to have considered himself lucky to escape execution, but instead contrived to regain control of Parthia and Hyrcania; ultimately, however, he was arrested and killed. The latter was reinstated in his old satrapy of Aria (in the Herat region of Afghanistan), though a detachment of 40 javelin-men under Anaxippus was sent with him to his capital of Artacoana. Satibarzanes promptly murdered his escort and openly rebelled, encouraged perhaps by reports of Bessus's usurpation.

Only two days after learning of Satibarzanes' treachery, Alexander was in Artacoana, from which the rebellious satrap had fled. But when Alexander replaced him with another native ruler, Arsaces, and moved on to subdue Afghanistan, Satibarzanes returned with the aim of reimposing his rule. In this he failed, and he was killed in single combat by the Macedonian cavalry officer Erigyius.

Alexander, meanwhile, moved south and came upon the Ariaspians, who lived near Lake Seistan. These supplied his army, just as 200 years earlier they had aided Cyrus the Great of Persia and earned the title *Euergetai* ('Benefactors'). From there the Macedonians followed the Helmand river valley, the course of which took them in the direction of Arachosia. A new settlement was established at Alexandria-in-Arachosia (near modern Kandahar), one of many such foundations in the area.

*The death of Satibarzanes*

'The deserter Satibarzanes commanded the barbarians. When he saw the battle flagging, with both sides equally matched in strength, he rode up to the front ranks, removed his helmet ... and challenged anyone willing to fight him in single combat, adding that he would remain bare-headed in the fight. Erigyius found the barbarian general's display of bravado intolerable. Though well advanced in age, Erigyius was not to be ranked second to any of the younger men in courage and agility. He took off his helmet and revealed his white hair ... One might have thought that an order to cease fighting had been given on both sides. At all events they immediately fell back, leaving an open space, eager to see how matters would turn out ...

The barbarian threw his spear first. Moving his head slightly to the side, Erigyius avoided it. Then, spurring on his horse, he brought up his lance and ran it straight through the barbarian's gullet, so that it projected through the back of his neck. The barbarian was thrown from his mount, but still fought on. Erigyius drew the spear from the wound and drove it again into his face. Satibarzanes grabbed it with his hand, aiding his enemy's stroke to hasten his own death.

Quintus Curtius Rufus, *History of Alexander* 7.4.33–37

In 329, Alexander again turned to deal with Bessus in Bactria, crossing the Hindu Kush via the Khawak Pass and reaching Qunduz. On his approach, the barbarians sent word that they were prepared to hand over to him the usurper Bessus; stripped naked, in chains and wearing a dog-collar, Bessus was left by the roadway to be picked up by Alexander's agent, Ptolemy. But those who had betrayed him fled, wary of submitting to Alexander and determined to maintain their independence in one of the most remote regions of the empire.

Bessus was sent to Ecbatana to be tortured and executed, the traditional punishment for traitors. He had done more than simply murder Darius; he had challenged Alexander's claims to the kingship. Claims to legitimacy have little force, however, unless backed by military action, as Darius's illustrious forefather and namesake had discovered in the years from 522 to 519. That king's imperial propaganda, inscribed in three languages on the rock face of Bisutun, proclaims how he became king through the will of Ahura-Mazda; but it took the might of his armies and the public execution of his opponents to confirm the god's will.

And so too Alexander was forced to fight on. Seven towns along the Iaxartes (Syr-Darya) offered stubborn resistance but fell to the conquerors, and at Cyropolis,

Modern Khojend. The city began as a settlement (Alexandria-Eschate) to protect the crossing of the Iaxartes river (Syr-Darya). In this vicinity Cyrus the Great had also established a frontier outpost. (TRIP)

founded by Cyrus the Great at the northern limit of his empire, the King was wounded in the neck. A new frontier settlement nearby – this one called Alexandria-Eschate ('Alexandria the Farthest', modern Khojend) – served to restrict the flow of the Scythian horsemen who were aiding the Bactrian rebels, but it threatened the patterns of life in Sogdiana and only incited further insurrections. A guerrilla war ensued, with the rebels entrusting their families and property to the numerous strongholds in the region.

One of the local barons, Sisimithres (known officially as Chorienes), took refuge on Koh-i-nor, which the ancients called simply the Rock of Chorienes. Although his mother pressed him to resist the invader, Sisimithres was persuaded to surrender. Alexander had sent to him another prominent Sogdianian named Oxyartes, who may well have reported how the rebel Arimazes had been captured with relative ease, despite the natural defences of his fortress, and punished with crucifixion.

Over the winter of 328/327 Sisimithres supplied Alexander's army with pack

*Alexander and Roxane*
  'Writers give the height of the rock of
Sisimithres as 15 stades, with 80 stades as
its circumference. On top, it is reportedly
flat and contains good soil, which can
support 500 men, and on it Alexander is
said to have been sumptuously
entertained and to have married Roxane,
the daughter of Oxyartes.'
Strabo, *Geography* 11.11.4

animals, sheep and cattle, as well as
2,000 camels. Alexander returned the favour
when spring approached, plundering the
territory of the Sacae and returning to
Sisimithres with 30,000 head of cattle. This
gesture, too, was matched by the barbarian,
who entertained him on the Rock. Here it
was that Alexander met Oxyartes' daughter,
Roxane, whom he subsequently married. It is
depicted as a love-match, which may be true,
but the political implications did not escape
Alexander either. By means of a wedding
ceremony, the Macedonian King terminated

*Tension between Alexander and his
Macedonians*
  Ever since the death of Darius,
Alexander had become increasingly
orientalised. He had begun to adopt
certain elements of Persian dress; his
belief in his divine parentage was also
regarded as an eastern pretension.
Furthermore, he had become more
autocratic. In summer 328 Alexander
killed Cleitus the Black, the man who
had saved his life at the Granicus, in a
drunken quarrel in Samarkand. In the
following spring, several pages along
with Hermolaus conspired to murder the
King, but their plot was revealed and the
conspirators were executed. Callisthenes,
the tutor of the pages, was suspected of
complicity and put to death as well.
And, in these years, the King had begun
to drink more heavily than before.

the lengthy guerrilla war that he had been
unable to bring to an end militarily. Philip II
had used political marriage to great
advantage in his time; after seven years of
campaigning, Alexander too had come to
appreciate its usefulness.

  It is difficult to determine how much the
marriage to Roxane influenced Alexander's
thinking about the benefits of intermarriage
with the barbarians. Some ancient writers
mention other marriages between
Macedonians and barbarian women at this
time, but these may anticipate the great
mass-marriage ceremony at Susa in 324. It is
certain, however, that soon after marrying
Roxane Alexander attempted to introduce
the Persian custom of obeisance (*proskynesis*)
at his court. This met with fierce resistance
on the part of his Macedonian generals and
courtiers, and the King reluctantly
abandoned the scheme.

## Invasion of India

The political marriage of Alexander and
Roxane had brought the guerrilla war in
Bactria and Sogdiana to an end, but the
fighting was to continue. The Macedonian
army now turned its attention to the last
corner of the Achaemenid Empire. Here
three provinces remained: Parapamisadae,
which lay beyond the passes of the Hindu
Kush as one marched east from the city of
Bactra (Balkh, near Masar-e-sharif); Gandhara
(now part of northern Pakistan); and
Hindush (Sindh), the valley of the Indus.
Once through the Hindu Kush, Alexander
advanced into the Bajaur and Swat regions,
moving relentlessly towards the Indus, where
an advance force under Hephaestion and
Perdiccas had constructed a boat-bridge
across the river, leading into the territory of
the Taxiles.

  On the march, Alexander had
encountered fierce resistance from the
Aspasians and Assacenians. The chief city of
the latter was Massaga, located in the Katgala
Pass and defended by a woman, Cleophis,
the mother (or possibly widow) of the local

The wedding of Alexander and Roxane. Painting by Il Sodoma, based on an ancient account of the painting by Aetion. (AKG Berlin)

### Perdiccas, son of Orontes

Perdiccas was another of the young and talented officers of Alexander, one of several who would struggle for power after the death of the King. In 336, he was a member of Philip II's hypaspist bodyguard: it was unfortunate that the King's assassination occurred 'on his shift', to use modern parlance. Alexander promoted him to the rank of taxiarch and as such he led one of the brigades of the *pezhetairoi*. Probably in 330, he became a member of the seven-man Bodyguard (*Somatophylakes*) and soon afterwards he commanded a hipparchy of the Companion Cavalry. He appears to have worked well with Alexander's closest friend, Hephaestion, but others found him difficult to deal with.

After Hephaestion's death, he was undoubtedly the most influential of the King's officers, and after Alexander's own death Perdiccas was the logical person to assume control of affairs in Babylon. Nevertheless, he had made too many enemies and his ambition made him the object of suspicion and hatred. In 320 BC his invasion of Egypt failed and he was murdered by his own officers.

dynast, Assacenus. He had died only shortly before Alexander's arrival at the city, probably in an earlier attempt to stop the Macedonians *en route*. It was Assacenus's brother, Amminais, who conducted the actual defence, with the help of 9,000 mercenaries, but legend chooses instead to focus on the Queen, who negotiated the surrender of the city and retained her throne

### Queen Cleophis of Massaga

'From there he headed for ... the realm of Queen Cleophis. She surrendered to Alexander but subsequently regained her throne, which she ransomed by sleeping with him, attaining by sexual favours what she could not by force of arms. The child fathered by the king she named Alexander, and he later rose to sovereignty over the Indians. Because she had thus degraded herself Queen Cleophis was from that time called the "royal whore" by the Indians.'
Justin 12.7.9–11 (J. C. Yardley trans., Clarendon Ancient History series)

Samarkand today. The old city of Maracanda occupied the mound behind the city. It was here that Alexander killed his friend and general Cleitus in a drunken brawl. (TRIP)

by dazzling Alexander with her beauty. Her story must be read with caution, since her name and conduct are reminiscent of the famous Egyptian queen, Cleopatra VII. The first historian to mention her may, indeed, have written in the Augustan age, when Cleopatra herself had gained notoriety.

Some of the Assacenians fled to a seemingly impregnable mountain known to the ancients as Aornus (probably Pir-sar, though some have suggested Mt Ilam). Here, just as he had done in his siege of Arimazes, Alexander overcame the rugged terrain, this time herding many of the terrified natives to their deaths as they attempted to descend the steep embankment overhanging the Indus. By capturing the place, the King could claim to have outdone his mythical ancestor, Hercules, who had been driven off by an earthquake.

The King now crossed into the territory of Ambhi (officially 'Taxiles'), who ruled the region between the Indus and Hydaspes (Jhelum) rivers and gave Alexander a lavish reception in his capital at Taxila (near modern Islamabad). He was at the time hard pressed by his enemies – Abisares to the north (in the Kashmir) and Porus, Rajah of the Paurava, to the west. In exchange for support, he accepted a Macedonian garrison and an overseer, Philip, son of Machatas. But Ambhi remained nominal head of the territory.

Porus meanwhile had urged Abisares to lend aid against Taxiles and the Macedonian invader. Instead, he made (token?) submission to Alexander, content to await the outcome of events. And when Porus went down to defeat, Abisares sent money and elephants, but argued that he could not come in person on account of illness. It is an old trick of rulers who are confronted by those more powerful, and it was attempted later by Montezuma when Cortés approached Tenochtitlán.

Porus himself determined to face the invader and his arch-enemy, Taxiles, at the Hydaspes river, guarding the crossing near modern Haranpur. There would be no repeat of the charge at the Granicus. The Hydaspes was a much greater river, the banks steeper, and the effect of the elephants stationed upon them decisive. It was necessary to make the crossing elsewhere, and to do so unopposed.

At first, Alexander resorted to a series of feints – or, more precisely, to a repetition of the same feint, as he marched a detachment

The battle between Alexander and Porus. In the battle at the Hydaspes river, Alexander and Porus did not actually meet each other in combat, although the Macedonian King met the Indian rajah after he had suffered numerous wounds. (Ann Ronan Picture Library)

*A digression on boat-bridges*
The historian Arrian can find no evidence for how Alexander bridged the Indus, but he comments: 'The quickest way of bridging I know is the Roman use of boats ... Their boats are at a signal allowed to float downstream, yet not bows on, but as if backing. The stream naturally carries them down, but a rowing skiff holds them up till it manoeuvres them into the appointed place and at that point wicker crates of pyramid shape full of unhewn stones are let down from the bows of each ship to hold it against the stream. No sooner has one ship thus been made fast than another, just at the right interval to carry the superstructure safely, is anchored upstream and from both boats timbers are accurately and smartly laid and planks crosswise to bind them together. The work goes on in this way for all the boats needed ... On either side of the bridge gangways are laid and fastened down, so that the passage may be safer for horses and baggage animals, and also to bind the bridge together.' Arrian 5.7.3–5 (P. A. Brunt trans., Loeb Classical Library)

of the army to a position upstream and returned again to the main camp, while Porus's forces on the opposite bank mirrored his actions. Soon he positioned a contingent under Meleager several miles to the north; but Porus too had taken precautions against

encirclement by instructing his brother, Spitaces, to keep watch upstream.

Craterus, with the heavy infantry, was left to face the main Indian army at the original crossing-point, and Alexander eventually, under the cover of night, heavy rain and thunder, marched some 17½ miles (28km) upriver (near modern Jalalpur) and made a crossing just where the heavily wooded island of Admana sits in a bend of the river. Here he reached the opposite side before Spitaces was able to challenge him. Indeed, the island had

proved to be such an effective screen that
Alexander himself landed his men there,
mistaking it for the opposite bank of the
Hydaspes. Consequently, Porus had to
abandon his original position and turn to meet
the encircling force, while Craterus began to
lead the rest of the army across the river.

The engagement that followed was decided
primarily by the cavalry, even though the
heavy rains had reduced the battlefield to
mud and swamp. The elephants, interspersed
between units of infantry, proved once again
to be a greater liability than advantage to
Porus's army. In the end, the Macedonians
were victorious. Porus had fought gallantly
and received many wounds.

The valiant enemy earned Alexander's
respect, and was allowed to retain his kingdom.
It had not always been so: Alexander had often
been less than generous in his treatment of
stubborn adversaries. (Witness the case of Batis
of Gaza, whom Alexander dragged behind his
chariot in imitation of Achilles' treatment of
Hector.) The greater challenge lay, however, in
the attempt to bring about lasting peace
between the Indian rivals. Curtius claims that
an alliance between Taxiles and Poros was
sealed by marriage, the common currency in
such transactions. But the arrangement was
never entirely satisfactory. Though Taxiles was
perhaps more to be trusted than Poros,
Alexander needed the latter for his upcoming
campaigns in the Punjab.

*Porus and Alexander*
Alexander was the first to speak.
'What,' he said, 'do you wish that I
should do with you?'
'Treat me as a king ought,' Porus is
said to have replied.
'For my part,' said Alexander, pleased
by the answer, 'your request shall be
granted. But is there not something you
would wish for yourself? Ask it.'
'Everything,' said Porus, 'is contained in
this one request.'
Arrian 5.19 (A. de Sélincourt
trans., Penguin)

## The limits of conquest

Victorious over the army of Porus, the
Macedonians had moved eastward across the
Punjab, coming inevitably to the Hyphasis
(Beas) river. Beyond this lay the populous and
little-known subcontinent of India proper. (It
should be noted that Alexander never crossed
the boundaries of what is modern India.) Here
it was that the war-weary Macedonians,
battered by the elements, their uniforms
literally rotting off their bodies, called a halt.
Alexander yearned for further adventure and
conquest, this time in the valley of the
Ganges. The soldiers, however, conducted a
strike (*secessio*) and even the bravest and most
loyal of Alexander's officers spoke on their
behalf. The King sulked in his tent, but the
men remained obdurate. There was nothing to
do but turn back.

This is the traditionally accepted view of
the end of Alexander's eastward march. But
did it really happen in this way? Why, one
asks, would an experienced and shrewd
military leader like Alexander allow reports
of extraordinary dangers, or numerous
enemies and exotic places, to come to the
attention of soldiers who, as he knew
perfectly well, were demoralised and tired?
The skilful leader tells his troops what he
wants them to know, which is virtually
always less than the whole truth. If the
fantastic report of India beyond the Hyphasis
was 'leaked' to the Macedonian soldiery, it
was because he wanted them to hear it. If it
was merely a case of rumour taking hold,
then Alexander handled the matter badly. In
his speech to the men, in which he claims to
be debunking the rumours, he nevertheless
reports them in vivid detail; then he changes
his tack and argues that, even if the stories
are true, there is no need to be concerned.

This was not the time for the truth, much
less for exaggeration. It was a face-saving
gesture by a king who was just as tired as his
men, for whom it would have been unheroic
to decline further challenges. Instead the
responsibility for ending this glorious march
into the unknown was placed squarely on
the shoulders of the common soldier. His

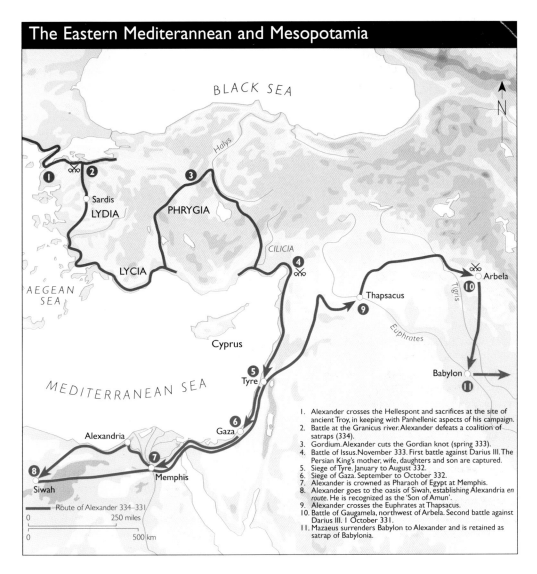

## The Eastern Mediterannean and Mesopotamia

BLACK SEA

N

Sardis
LYDIA
PHRYGIA
Halys
CILICIA
LYCIA
AEGEAN SEA
Arbela
Tigris
Thapsacus
Cyprus
Euphrates
Babylon
MEDITERRANEAN SEA
Tyre
Gaza
Alexandria
Memphis
Siwah

Route of Alexander 334–331
0                     250 miles
0                              500 km

1. Alexander crosses the Hellespont and sacrifices at the site of ancient Troy, in keeping with Panhellenic aspects of his campaign.
2. Battle at the Granicus river. Alexander defeats a coalition of satraps (334).
3. Gordium. Alexander cuts the Gordian knot (spring 333).
4. Battle of Issus. November 333. First battle against Darius III. The Persian King's mother, wife, daughters and son are captured.
5. Siege of Tyre. January to August 332.
6. Siege of Gaza. September to October 332.
7. Alexander is crowned as Pharaoh of Egypt at Memphis.
8. Alexander goes to the oasis of Siwah, establishing Alexandria en route. He is recognized as the 'Son of Amun'.
9. Alexander crosses the Euphrates at Thapsacus.
10. Battle of Gaugamela, northwest of Arbela. Second battle against Darius III. 1 October 331.
11. Mazaeus surrenders Babylon to Alexander and is retained as satrap of Babylonia.

stubbornness alone robbed Alexander of further glory. This was the propaganda line, and this is how it has come down to us. Further evidence of Alexander's duplicity can be found in the fact that he ordered the men to build a camp of abnormal size, containing artefacts that were larger than life, in order to cheat posterity into thinking that the expeditionary force had been superhuman.

## Return to the west

The army was returning to the west – but not directly. It was not necessary to cross the Hyphasis in the quest for ocean. Alexander knew full well that the Indus river system would lead him there, and he had transported boats in sections for the very purpose of following the river to its mouth. On the way, he subdued warlike tribes, troublesome neighbours for his new vassal, Porus. Among these were the Mallians, in whose town Alexander would have a close brush with death.

Disregarding his own safety and forgetting that the Macedonians' enthusiasm for war was no longer what it had been, Alexander was the first to scale the city walls and jump inside. Only a few bodyguards accompanied him. When the troops saw that their King was trapped, they scrambled up the ladders, overloading and breaking them. Inside the walls, the King was showered with arrows: one protector at least perished in his defence, while others were as gravely wounded as Alexander himself. Once the troops poured over the battlements, the slaughter began, but their King had an arrow lodged deep in his chest, just below the ribs.

Miraculously, Alexander survived, though for a good portion of the journey downriver he was all but incapacitated. By the time he reached the Indus delta, he had recovered, and from here he sailed out into the Indian Ocean and conducted sacrifices at the limits of his empire, just as he had done at the Hellespont in 334.

Nevertheless, the return of the Macedonian army can hardly be depicted as triumphant. One portion sailed along the coast, eventually passing through the Straits of Hormuz and entering the Persian Gulf: it was a journey fraught with hardship, deprivation and danger. Another, led by Alexander himself, struggled through the Gedrosian desert, suffering staggering losses on account of the elements and the malfeasance of the neighbouring satraps. Although Alexander

stood up to the hardships as well as any man, and indeed it was on this march that he displayed some of his most noble qualities, the march was an unmitigated disaster. Those modern writers who delight in blackening his reputation have gone so far as to suggest that Alexander exposed his men to the perils of the Gedrosian wasteland in order to pay them back for their refusal to proceed beyond the Hyphasis.

When Alexander returned to the west, he celebrated mixed marriages on a grand scale at Susa (324 BC). Alexander himself married Stateira, daughter of Darius III, and Parysatis, whose father, Artaxerxes III, had ruled shortly before. Another of Darius's daughters, Drypetis, married Hephaestion, and nearly a hundred other noble Persian women were given as brides to Macedonian officers. Even larger numbers of common soldiers took barbarian wives, but this was probably just a way of legitimising common-law unions that had existed for some time. The marriages appear to have been unpopular with the aristocracy, and after Alexander's death most appear to have repudiated their Persian wives.

On the other hand, it was the integration of large numbers of barbarian troops into the Macedonian army that gave offence to the soldiery. Not long afterwards, at Opis on the Tigris, the army mutinied, complaining that

Alexander wearing the elephant headdress. (AKG Berlin)

*Craterus, Alexander's most trusted commander*

Craterus began the expedition as a taxiarch, a commander of *pezhetairoi*. He served as the second-in-command on the left wing, under the direct authority of Parmenion, whom he was being groomed to replace. Craterus was an officer of unswerving loyalty to the King. The saying went that Hephaestion was 'fond of Alexander' (*philalexandros*) but Craterus was 'fond of the king' (*philobasileus*). Not surprisingly, these two young commanders would become rivals and their disagreements would lead to an open confrontation that threatened to involve their respective units. But Craterus's promotion was based on ability, whereas in Hephaestion's case there was at least a suspicion of nepotism – even if no one said so publicly.

As the campaign progressed, Craterus exercised more frequent independent commands. When Alexander returned through the Gedrosian desert, Craterus led the slower troops and the invalids through the Bolan Pass towards modern Kandahar. *En route* he apprehended rebels, whom he brought to the King for execution. In 324 he was sent to replace Antipater as viceroy of Macedon. This order would be pre-empted by Alexander's death and the outbreak of the Lamian War. In 321/320 Craterus returned to Asia and did battle with Eumenes near the Hellespont. He was, however, thrown from his horse and trampled beneath its hoofs. It was an ignominious end for one of Alexander's greatest generals.

they were being supplanted by foreigners. These complaints Alexander countered with soothing words, but the ringleaders of the mutiny were seized, chained and thrown into the Tigris. Ten thousand veterans, many of them injured, were sent back to Macedonia under the command of Craterus, who was himself in poor health. Some of them would indeed reach their homeland, but only to fight some more. Others would not advance beyond Cilicia before becoming embroiled in the wars of the Successors.

## Battle of the Hydaspes

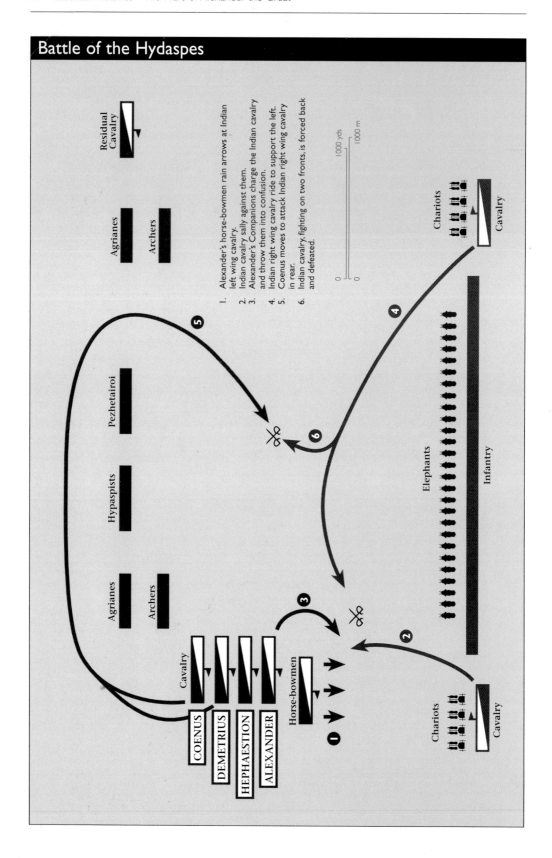

1. Alexander's horse-bowmen rain arrows at Indian left wing cavalry.
2. Indian cavalry sally against them.
3. Alexander's Companions charge the Indian cavalry and throw them into confusion.
4. Indian right wing cavalry ride to support the left.
5. Coenus moves to attack Indian right wing cavalry in rear.
6. Indian cavalry, fighting on two fronts, is forced back and defeated.

# Alexander's campaigns

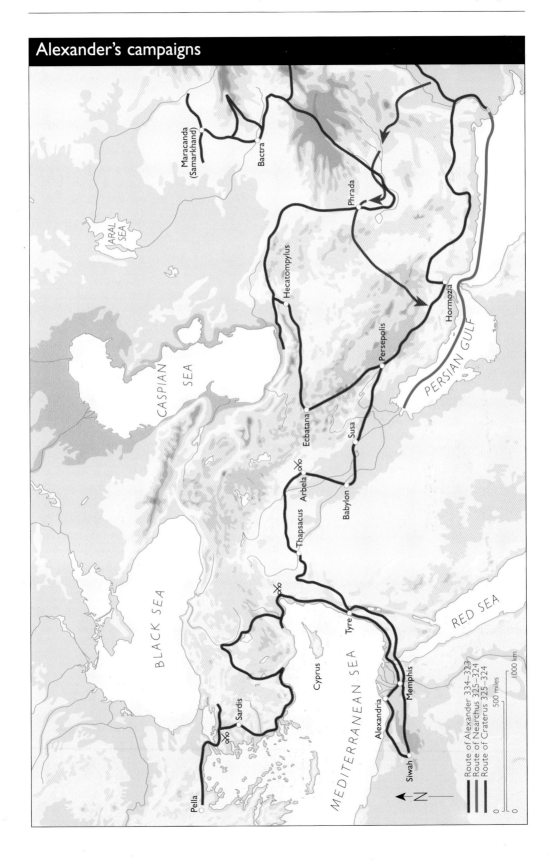

Maracanda (Samarkhand)

Bactra

Phrada

Hecatompylus

ARAL SEA

CASPIAN SEA

Hormozia

Persepolis

PERSIAN GULF

Ecbatana

Susa

Arbela

Thapsacus

Babylon

BLACK SEA

Tyre

RED SEA

Cyprus

Memphis

Sardis

Alexandria

MEDITERRANEAN SEA

Siwah

Pella

Route of Alexander 334–323
Route of Nearchus 325–324
Route of Craterus 325–324

1000 km

500 miles

N

# Two generals and a satrap

## Parmenion and Philotas

When Alexander ascended the Macedonian throne, two powerful generals of Philip II exercised considerable influence at the court and in the army. Only one, Antipater, was in Macedonia at the time. The other, Parmenion, had been sent by Philip to command the advance force in Asia Minor. He was an experienced and well-loved leader of men. In the year of Alexander's birth, 356 BC, Parmenion had defeated the Illyrian ruler Grabus, while Philip himself was besieging Potidaea. Twenty years later, he was the senior officer in the army and his sons, Philotas and Nicanor, commanded the Companion Cavalry and the hypaspists respectively. These were amongst the finest troops in the Macedonian army.

Parmenion's contributions were, however, a source of embarrassment to the young king, who believed that the success of others detracted somehow from his own glory. And he was particularly annoyed when he learned that in Egypt Parmenion's son, Philotas, was boasting that all the King's successes were due to his father's generalship.

The information had come to Alexander in an unusual way. Amongst the spoils taken at Damascus was a woman named Antigone. This woman was of Macedonian origin, from the town of Pydna, but had been captured by the Persian admiral Autophradates while travelling by sea to celebrate the mysteries of Samothrace. (It was at this festival, many years earlier, that Philip had met the young Olympias, the future mother of Alexander.) Antigone had thus become the mistress or concubine of a Persian notable and had been deposited at Damascus before the battle of Issus.

When Parmenion captured the city and the spoils were divided, Antigone became Philotas's mistress. What he told her, by way

of bragging about his own family's achievements or disparaging those of the King, she repeated to others, until the talk was reported to Craterus, a faithful friend and officer of Alexander. Craterus disliked Philotas personally – and in this he was not alone, for Philotas had many enemies who were at the same time close friends of the King. Craterus therefore gathered incriminating evidence from Antigone and brought this to Alexander's attention. But, at that time, with the outcome of the war against Darius still undecided, the King chose to overlook the indiscretion.

Things changed, however, when Alexander found himself master of the Persian capitals. Parmenion had suddenly become expendable, and he was left at Ecbatana when Alexander pushed on in pursuit of Darius and Bessus. At first, it was to be a temporary measure, but Darius's murder altered the complexion of the campaign. The Thessalian cavalry, which had served on Parmenion's wing, was now dismissed and sent back to Europe. And Craterus, who had been groomed as Parmenion's replacement – at both Issus and Gaugamela he was the old general's second-in-command – had proved himself more than capable; furthermore, he was younger, more energetic and, what was most important, unswervingly loyal to the King. These circumstances, and the fact that Parmenion's elimination required justification, gave rise to stories that Parmenion's advice was timid or unsound and that his performance at Gaugamela was substandard.

Separated from his influential father, Philotas became more vulnerable to the intrigues of his enemies. And this vulnerability was increased when, during the march through Aria, Philotas's brother

Nicanor died of illness. Indeed, not only was the family itself weakened, but also many who had served with Parmenion were no longer with the army. Hence, when Philotas was implicated in a conspiracy at Phrada (modern Farah) in Afghanistan in late 330, there were few to defend or protect him.

The crime itself was one of negligence rather than overt treason. A young Macedonian – he is described as one of the *hetairoi*, and hence not insignificant – by the name of Dimnus had divulged the details of a conspiracy to which he was a party (though he was clearly not its instigator), to his lover, Nicomachus. The latter, fearing for his life if the conspiracy should fail and he be implicated, told everything he knew to his brother, Cebalinus, who promptly went to report the matter to Alexander.

Unable to gain access to the King, Cebalinus informed Philotas and urged him to deal with the matter. But on the following day, when he approached Philotas again, Cebalinus discovered that the latter had not spoken to the King concerning the conspiracy because, as he claimed, it had not seemed to him a matter of great importance. Cebalinus therefore devised other means of revealing the plot, mentioning also Philotas's suspicious behaviour.

Alexander thus called a meeting of his advisers – excluding Philotas, who might otherwise have been summoned – and asked for their candid opinions. These were freely given and unanimous: Philotas would not have suppressed the information unless he were either party to the plot or at least favoured it. Such negligence could not be excused when it involved the life and safety of the King. And so Atarrhias with a detachment of hypaspists – in effect, these were the Macedonian military police – was sent to arrest Philotas.

Confronted with the facts, Philotas confessed that he had indeed learned of the conspiracy, but that he had not taken it seriously. If this was the truth – we shall never know what went through Philotas's mind – he may have reflected on an earlier episode, when his father had sent an urgent letter to Alexander, alleging that Philip of Acarnania, the King's personal physician, had been bribed to poison him in Cilicia. In the event, the report proved false and Parmenion's reputation was tarnished.

On the other hand, in the shadowy world of the Macedonian court, where kings had often been murdered for merely slighting a man's honour, anything was possible and everything potentially dangerous. Philotas's trustworthiness was called into question: had he not been guilty of disloyal talk in the past? As a young man, he had been raised at the court of Philip as a companion of Amyntas, son of Perdiccas, whom Alexander had executed on suspicion of aspiring to regain his throne. Furthermore, his sister had been married briefly to the King's bitter enemy Attalus.

When questioned under torture, Philotas admitted also that another adherent of Attalus, a certain squadron commander (*ilarches*) named Hegelochus had suggested to Parmenion and his sons that they murder the King; but the plan was rejected as too dangerous in the circumstances of 331. At any rate, it seems that the topic of Alexander's removal from power had certainly come up.

The younger commanders urged the King not to forgive Philotas a second time, for he

Alexander, as portrayed on the Alexander Sarcophagus, which shows his victory at Issus. (AKG Berlin)

would continue to be a danger to him. Their professed concern for Alexander's safety masked, only slightly, their hatred for Philotas and their desire for military advancement; this could best be achieved by eliminating him and members of his faction. For Alexander, although he concurred with their opinion, it was nevertheless a difficult decision. How would Parmenion react to his son's execution? He remained in Ecbatana, astride the lines of communication and at the head of a substantial army. If Philotas were to be executed for treason, then the charge must be extended to include his father. The army, which tried Philotas and found him guilty, accepted also the guilt of his father. The Macedonians were realists and recognised that expediency must triumph over legal niceties.

Philotas was publicly executed; his father in Ecbatana was presented with a letter outlining the charges against him and struck down as he read them.

## Mazaeus, servant of three kings

Mazaeus is known from both historical sources and coin legends to have been satrap of Cilicia, and later of Syria and Mesopotamia (Abarnahara, 'the land beyond the river') in the time of King Artaxerxes III. Under Darius III he had doubtless fought at Issus, although there is no mention of him. In 331, he had been ordered to prevent Alexander's crossing of the Euphrates at Thapsacus, but had insufficient numbers to do more than harass the bridge-builders. Upon Alexander's arrival, Mazaeus withdrew and rejoined Darius, who was now following the course of the Tigris northward.

At Gaugamela Mazaeus commanded the Persian cavalry on the right wing and led a charge of dense squadrons together with the scythe-chariots, inflicting heavy casualties. He then sent a squadron of Scythian horsemen to capture the Macedonian camp, while he himself exerted pressure on Parmenion and the Thessalian cavalry on the Macedonian left. Parmenion, in turn, was forced to send riders to recall Alexander, who

*A missed opportunity*

'The [Macedonian] army could have been annihilated if anyone had had the courage to seize victory at this juncture, but the King's unceasing good fortune kept the enemy at bay ... If Mazaeus had attacked the Macedonians as they crossed [the Tigris], he would no doubt have defeated them while they were in disorder, but he began to ride towards them only when they were on the bank and already under arms. He had sent only 1,000 cavalry ahead, and so Alexander, discovering and then scorning their small numbers, ordered Ariston, the commander of the Paeonian cavalry, to charge them at full gallop.' Quintus Curtius Rufus, *The History of Alexander* 4.9.22–24

had gone off in pursuit of Darius. Eventually Mazaeus was overcome by the tenacity of the Thessalians and the demoralising news of Darius's flight.

It is highly likely that the great battle-scene on the so-called Alexander Sarcophagus from Sidon – now in the Istanbul Museum – depicts Mazaeus's valour. If this is so, then, contrary to the accepted modern scholarly view, the sarcophagus itself would have been commissioned for the former satrap of Syria (and resident of Sidon) rather than the undistinguished Abdalonymus, whom Hephaestion had elevated to the kingship in 332.

Mazaeus fled from the battlefield to Babylon, which he promptly surrendered to the Macedonians. In return he was installed as its satrap, the first Persian to be so honoured by Alexander. (Mithrenes had been in Alexander's entourage since 334, but his appointment as satrap of Armenia did not occur until 330.) The Alexander Sarcophagus also depicts a notable Persian engaged in a lion hunt together with Alexander and other Macedonians – one of the Macedonian riders may be Hephaestion. If this depicts a historical event, then it could not have occurred before late 331, and the most likely Persian with whom Alexander hunted is once again Mazaeus.

When Alexander pursued Darius in his final days, Mazaeus's son, Brochubelus or Antibelus, defected to him. Mazaeus himself remained in office and served his new master loyally until his death in late 328, whereupon he was replaced by another barbarian: Arrian calls the successor 'Stamenes' and Quintus Curtius Rufus writes, 'Ditamenes', but neither form is convincing.

# Rome, Carthage and India

## Emergence of Rome

The fourth century BC, which is treated by Greek historians as a period of decline after the so-called 'Golden Age of Athens', was for the Roman world a time of rebirth. The city which, according to its historical traditions, was founded in 753 BC – that is, 244 years before the establishment of the Republic in 509 – had experienced a period of growth in the fifth century that was arrested, indeed shattered, by the irruption of Gauls in 390 or 386. Despite face-saving propaganda that saw Camillus snatch victory from the grasp of the Gauls after they had defeated the Romans at the river Allia, the truth is that the Romans paid the marauders in order to be rid of them. The conquest of the Italian peninsula had to be started anew, if indeed much of it had been subject to Rome before the Gallic sack.

At about the same time as Alexander crossed into Asia, his uncle and brother-in-law, Alexander I of Epirus, crossed the Adriatic in order to champion the cause of the Greeks in southern Italy, who were being hard pressed by the Lucanians and Bruttians. Roman historians later commented on the Epirote King's failure, noting that 'whereas Alexander the Great had been fighting *women* in Asia, the other Alexander had encountered *men*'. This unflattering remark was typical of Roman attitudes towards Alexander the Great, for it was a popular topic of debate whether Alexander would have been able to conquer the Romans.

Later Hellenistic kings, like Philip V, Antiochus III and Perseus, proved to be unworthy of Alexander's reputation, and the Romans themselves, or at least those who were honest with themselves, knew that these were pale reflections of a bygone era.

Indeed, Pyrrhus, a second cousin of the conqueror, was destined to give the Romans a fright some 43 years after Alexander's death. And his was but a small army, with limited goals.

Alexander of Epirus, however, suffered the fate of all champions summoned by the Italian Greeks: rather than joining him in the struggle against their enemies, they were content to sit back and let him do the fighting for them. Ultimately, he was killed – the victim of a prophesied fate that he had gone to Italy to avoid. The oracle of Dodona had foretold that he would die by the Acheron river. Since there was a river of this name in Epirus, Alexander decided to move on to Italy, only to discover as he was struck down in an Italian stream that it too was known as the Acheron.

Such at least is the legend and the bitter lesson that those who seek to avert fortune must learn. But the important fact is that, as Alexander the Great was subduing the east, his namesake was engaged in a struggle between the inhabitants of the western peninsula who had not yet fallen under the power of Rome. But this was soon to come. In the years that followed, the Romans defeated the Samnites in three bitter wars, and by 265, seven years after the death of Pyrrhus, they were confronting the Carthaginians across the straits of Messina. When Alexander the Great died in Babylon, the First Punic War was only two generations in the future (see *The Punic Wars* in this series).

## Carthage

Carthage, the North African city near modern Tunis, was founded according to tradition in 814/813 by settlers from Tyre: the name Kart-Hadasht is Phoenician for 'New Town'.

Although archaeological evidence has yet to confirm the traditional date, it certainly existed by the late eighth century and soon developed as the most important Phoenician settlement in the western Mediterranean. Its proximity to Sicily, where numerous Phoenician trading posts (*emporia*) had been established, made it a natural protector of the Punic peoples against the Greeks of the island.

By Alexander's time, Carthaginian power had been restricted to western Sicily, but it was to become a serious threat to the city of Syracuse by the last decade of the fourth century. Not much later Carthage became embroiled in a struggle with Rome, as a result of an appeal to both parties by a group of lawless mercenaries, the Mamartines (or 'Sons of Mars'), who had taken over Messana, across from the toe of Italy.

That incident led to the First Punic War (264–241), which forced the Romans to develop a real navy for the first time in their history – along with the effective but ephemeral device known as the *corvus* or

*The fate of Alexander of Epirus*

'Alexander, king of Epirus, had been invited into Italy when the people of Tarentum petitioned his aid against the Bruttii. He had embarked on the expedition enthusiastically, as though a partition of the world had been made, the East being allotted to Alexander, son of his sister Olympias, and the West to himself, and believing he would have no less scope to prove himself in Italy, Africa and Sicily than Alexander was going to have in Asia and Persia. There was a further consideration. Just as the Delphic Oracle had forewarned Alexander the Great of a plot against him in Macedonia, so an oracular response from Jupiter at Dodona had warned this Alexander against the city of Pandosia and the Acherusian River; and since both were in Epirus – and he was unaware that identically-named places existed in Italy – he had been all the more eager to opt for a campaign abroad, in order to avoid the perils of destiny … He commenced hostilities with both the Bruttii and the Lucanians, capturing many of their cities, and he concluded treaties and alliances with the Metapontines, the Poediculi and the Romans. The Bruttii and the Lucanians, however, gathered auxiliary forces from their neighbours and resumed their war with increased fervour. During this campaign the king was killed in the vicinity of Pandosia and the River Acheron. He did not discover the name of the fateful region until he fell, and only when he was dying did he realize that the death which had led him to flee his native land had not threatened him there after all. The people of Thurii ransomed and buried his body at public expense.' Justin 12.2.1–5, 12–15 (J.C. Yardley trans., Clarendon Ancient History series)

Bronze head of Alexander from the third century BC. (Madrid, Prado)

Persian illustration of Alexander talking to wise men. (Ann
Ronan Picture Library)

Dionysus on a leopard. Mosaic from Pella, 4th century BC. When Alexander reached India he began to emulate Dionysus as well as Heracles, the paternal ancestor he had venerated since the beginning of his reign. (Archaeological Museum of Thessaloniki)

korax, a beaked grappling device attached to a boarding platform. It also led them to acquire their first provinces outside Italy. But it was the first of a series of life-and-death struggles between the two dominant states of

*Alexander learns of the Nanda rulers*
'Porus ... added that their ruler was not merely a commoner but a man from the lowest class. His father had been a barber whose regular employment barely kept starvation at bay, but by his good looks he had won the heart of the queen. By her he had been brought into a comparatively close friendship with the king of the time, whom he then treacherously murdered, seizing the throne ostensibly as protector of the king's children. He then killed the children and sired this present ruler, who had earned the hatred and contempt of the people by behaviour more in keeping with his father's station in life than his own.'
Curtius 9.2.6–7 (J. C. Yardley trans., Penguin)

the west. This would see the emergence of a general who was, in many ways, the equal of Alexander: Hannibal, the avowed 'enemy of Rome'. But when Alexander was conquering the east, the bitter Punic Wars and the brilliance of Hannibal and Scipio were still in the unforeseen future.

## India and the Mauryan dynasty

In the east, meanwhile, in the valley of the Ganges, the Nanda dynasty was nearing its end. Rumour held that the ruling king, whom the Greeks called Xandrames, was the son of a lowly barber who had murdered his sovereign and married the Queen. Plutarch, in his *Life of Alexander*, comments that when the Macedonians reached the Punjab they were seen by a young man named Sandracottus, who was destined to be the founder of the Mauryan dynasty and was known to the Indians as Chandragupta. He would later force Alexander's successor in the east, Seleucus Nicator, to cede the satrapies adjacent to the Indus in return for 500 elephants. But in the mid-320s, much of India was ripe for the picking.

## The Galatians

Far to the north and the west of Greece, another group, the Celts or Gauls, were beginning a steady migration eastward that would lead them down the Balkan river valleys towards Macedonia. In the years that followed 280, they would throw Macedonia and northern Greece into turmoil. One column would advance as far as Delphi, only to be driven off (seemingly with the aid of Apollo) by the Aetolians, who were hailed as saviours of Greece. According to their own tradition, they were beaten by their own drunkenness and lack of discipline. Eventually, they were transported across the Bosporus and came to settle in north-central Anatolia in the region that bears their name, Galatia. For the next century they would be the scourge of Asia Minor.

# A historian, athletes and courtesans

## Callisthenes the historian

Callisthenes of Olynthus was, according to some accounts, the nephew of the philosopher Aristotle, and although he is often depicted as a philosopher himself, he was little more than an amateur. He joined Alexander's expedition as the official historian and, if – as appears to be the case – he sent his history back to European Greece in instalments, he was at the same time historian, propagandist and war correspondent.

His travels with Alexander took him to exotic places and he was able to speculate on natural phenomena as well as describe the course of the war, for he appears to have theorised about the source of the Nile. It was his literary training that led him to depict Alexander as a latter-day Achilles, and it would not be wrong to class him with the numerous flatterers who swelled the King's ego and entourage. But, although he likened the receding sea near Mt Climax in Pamphylia to a courtier doing obeisance (*proskynesis*) to the Great King, he nevertheless resisted Alexander's attempt to introduce the Persian court protocol in 328/327. For this reason, he fell out with the King and when, some time later, a conspiracy was uncovered involving the royal pages, Callisthenes was easily implicated.

It was one of his functions at the court to tutor the young men of the Macedonian aristocracy – just as in the 340s Aristotle had tutored Alexander and several of his coeval friends (*syntrophoi*) at Mieza. Abrupt and austere in manner, Callisthenes had made few friends, though some like Lysimachus the Bodyguard may have enjoyed exchanging philosophical ideas with him. These two 'serious types' may have 'bonded', as modern jargon would have it, for Lysimachus's personality can hardly be termed effervescent.

Convicted of complicity in the conspiracy of the pages, Callisthenes was apparently incarcerated and died some months later of obesity and a disease of lice. The Peripatetic philosophers, the followers of Aristotle, never forgave Alexander.

> *Callisthenes defies Alexander*
> Alexander sent around a loving cup of gold, first to those with whom he had made an agreement about obeisance (*proskynesis*); the first who drank from it rose, did obeisance, and received a kiss from Alexander, and this went round all in turn. But when the pledge came to Callisthenes, he rose, drank from the cup, went up to Alexander and made to kiss him without having done obeisance. At that moment Alexander was talking to Hephaestion and therefore was not attending to see whether the ceremony of obeisance was carried out ... But as Callisthenes approached to kiss Alexander, Demetrius, son of Pythonax, one of the Companions, remarked that he was coming without having done obeisance. Alexander did not permit Callisthenes to kiss him; and Callisthenes remarked: 'I shall go away short one kiss.'
> Arrian 4.12.4–5 (P. A. Brunt trans., Loeb Classical Library, slightly modified)

## Flatterers and professional athletes

The entourage of the Macedonian King included a wide variety of non-combatants. Actors and musicians, poets and dancers, jugglers and ball-players can all be found in Alexander's camp, though many of them made only brief stops with the army as they toured the Greek cities of the Near East. Actors were particularly useful: because they travelled and because they spoke so eloquently, they were often used as envoys to the court of some king or dynast; sometimes they merely brought news of events in another part of the empire. Thus Alexander received news of the defection of his treasurer Harpalus from Cissus and Ephialtes, two comic actors who are attested as winners in dramatic competitions in Athens.

Some actors were clearly present at the Hydaspes river, for it was there that the troops were entertained with a production of the comic play *Agen*, written by a certain Python – possibly of Sicilian origin. Another actor, Thersippus, carried Alexander's letter to Darius, rejecting the King's offer to ransom the members of his family, whom Alexander had captured at Issus. And, at the drinking party in Maracanda (Samarkand) there were bards who sang of a Macedonian battle in the region. We are not told what it was they sang about, except that it was a Macedonian defeat. One scholar has plausibly suggested that they had produced a mock heroic epic that recounted the valour of one of their own, the harpist Aristonicus, who fought valiantly and died when barbarian horsemen attacked a small contingent of Macedonians, including pages and non-combatants.

Athletes are also attested in the camp. A young man named Serapion appears to have served no useful purpose other than to play ball with the King. But most famous of the athletes was an Athenian boxer, Dioxippus, who is named also as one of the King's flatterers. The confrontation in India between a Macedonian soldier, Corrhagus, and the Greek athlete reveals not only the ethnic tension that existed in the army between Greeks and Macedonians, but also the typical disdain of the veteran soldier for the professional athlete. Both men had imbibed excessively and, after they had exchanged insults, the Macedonian challenged the Athenian to a duel. This was fought on the

*A Greek boxer in Alexander's entourage: a warrior's opinion of a professional athlete*
'One person present at the banquet was the Athenian Dioxippus, a former boxer whose superlative strength had rendered him well known and well liked by Alexander. Jealous and spiteful men would make cutting remarks about him, partly in jest, partly in earnest, saying that they had along with them a useless, bloated animal and that, while they went into battle, he was dripping with oil and preparing his belly for a banquet. Now at this feast the Macedonian Horratas, who was already drunk, began to make the same type of insulting comment to Dioxippus and to challenge him, if he were a man, to fight a duel with him with swords the next day. Only then, said Horratas, would Alexander be able to decide whether he was reckless or Dioxippus a coward.'
Q. Curtius Rufus, *The History of Alexander* 9.7.16–17 (J. C Yardley trans., Penguin)

following day, with the athlete getting the better of the soldier. But Dioxippus's success did not endear him to the King, and soon afterwards he was framed by certain courtiers, who planted a drinking cup in his quarters and claimed that he had stolen it from one of the King's parties. Dishonoured by this trick, Dioxippus committed suicide, the victim of two forms of prejudice.

## Courtesans: Thaïs, Pythionice and Glycera

The presence of prostitutes has been a feature of armies since the earliest time. Even the Crusader armies, motivated by the most righteous intentions, had no shortage of them. Alexander himself certainly had the occasional liaison with such women: Pancaste had been the mistress of Alexander before he gave her to the painter Apelles, who had fallen in love with her.

Whether the Athenian courtesan Thaïs was originally Alexander's mistress before she took up with Ptolemy is unclear. The popular account of Alexander (the so-called Vulgate) portrays her as the one who, when revelling with the King in Persepolis, induced him to put the torch to the royal palace. But she is not some fictitious character, invented to discredit the King. At some point she became the mistress of Ptolemy and bore him three children – Lagus, Leontiscus and Eirene – the first named after Ptolemy's father, the last destined to become the bride of Eunostus, the King of Soli on Cyprus.

Most notorious, however, were the Athenian courtesans Pythionice and Glycera. They were in succession the mistresses of the treasurer Harpalus, who grieved excessively at the death of the former, and who allegedly built monuments for her, in Babylon and Athens, which surpassed those of great politicians and generals. The latter, Glycera, was treated by Harpalus as if she were a queen. He erected statues of himself and Glycera in Syria, and according to a hostile tradition made the people perform *proskynesis* in front of her.

*Theopompus denounces Harpalus to Alexander*

'Theopompus says, in his treatise *On the Chian Letter*, that after the death of Pythionice Harpalus summoned Glycera from Athens; on her arrival she took up her residence in the palace at Tarsus and had obeisance done to her by the populace, being hailed as queen; further, all persons were forbidden to honour Harpalus with a crown unless they also gave a crown to Glycera. In Rhossus they even went so far as to set up an image of her in bronze beside his own. The like is recorded by Cleitarchus in his *History of Alexander*.'

Athenaeus 13.586c (C. B. Gulick trans., Loeb Classical Library)

# The death of Alexander

The war against the barbarians of the east had, in fact, several different endings. The Panhellenic crusade, which was the pretext for going to war in the first place and the justification for the recruitment of allied Greek troops, came to an end in 330 BC, with the symbolic destruction of Persepolis and, later in Hyrcania, with the death of Darius. Those allied soldiers who wished to return home were dismissed from Hecatompylus. But the war itself was not yet finished. First, there was the matter of Bessus, who had usurped the throne: he wore the tiara upright, in the style of the Great King, and called himself Artaxerxes V. Secondly, there was the matter of annexing the remainder of the Persian Empire, which required Alexander to campaign as far north as the Syr-Darya (the Iaxartes river) and as far east as the Indus. And, when all this had been done, there was the task of consolidating his conquests.

But one thing had the effect of bringing Alexander's wars to an abrupt and permanent end: his premature death in Babylon. Those stories about seers warning him to avoid Babylon and omens of others occupying his throne are all inventions after the fact. Even the cause of his death was debated in ancient times and continues to be today. Was it typhoid, cholera or malaria? A good case has recently been made for the last one. Did he die of poison, the victim of a conspiracy by a number of his generals? This too gains support from the occasional modern historian, though the story of his murder was clearly a fabrication of the propaganda wars of his successors. Or was he the victim of depression and alcoholism? This is the most difficult to prove, since we cannot psychoanalyse him or determine to what extent his drinking affected his health. The Macedonians were notoriously heavy

drinkers, by ancient standards at least, and there are tales of drinking contests in which the winner does not live long enough to enjoy the prize. In fact, the stories of alcoholism are suspect as well: they were invented, or at least embellished, by writers like Ephippus of Olynthus with the aim of discrediting the King.

This is what we do know. After sailing on the marshes of the Euphrates waterway near Babylon, a region where malaria was endemic, the King returned to the city. One evening he was invited to a drinking party at the home of Medius of Larisa. While drinking, he suddenly experienced a pain in his chest, 'as if he had been pierced by an arrow or a spear'. He soon returned to his own quarters and his health deteriorated steadily. Nevertheless, he slept, bathed and continued drinking, at least for a while. He developed a fever, which became more severe, and not long afterwards he began to lose the ability to speak. By the time the men had learned of his predicament, he was not longer able to address them, but could only make physical gestures of recognition. On 10 or 11 June 323, he was dead. He had not yet reached his thirty-third birthday.

The loss of a dearly loved king was bad enough, but the uncertainty of the future was increased by the fact that no provisions had been made for the succession and numerous controversial policies had been set in motion – the proclamation of the Exiles' Decree, which had a disruptive effect on the politics of the Greek world, and the orders that Craterus should relieve Antipater of his command in Europe. Grandiose and expensive plans had also been laid, both for the erection of monuments (e.g. the massive funeral pyre for Hephaestion) and for military expeditions. It soon became clear that, although the conquests had come to an end, the war was about to be prolonged; for the struggles between Alexander's marshals were destined to be more bitter and more destructive than those against the Persian enemy.

*The Persian Queen Mother learns of Alexander's death*

'The news quickly reached Darius' mother too. She ripped off the clothes she wore and assumed the dress of mourning; she tore her hair and flung herself to the ground. Next to her sat one of her granddaughters who was in mourning after the recent loss of her husband, Hephaestion, and the general anguish reminded her of her personal grief. But Sisygambis alone felt the woes that engulfed her entire family: she wept for her own plight and that of her granddaughters. The fresh pain had also reminded her of the past. One might have thought that Darius was recently lost and that at the same time the poor woman had to bury two sons. She wept simultaneously for the living and the dead. Who would look after her girls, she wondered? Who would be another Alexander? This meant a second captivity, a second loss of royal status. On the death of Darius they had found a protector, but after Alexander they would certainly not find someone to guard their interests.

... Finally, she surrendered to her sorrow. She covered her head, turned away from her granddaughter and grandson, who fell at her knees to plead with her, and withdrew simultaneously from nourishment and daylight. Five days after deciding on death, she expired.' Quintus Curtius Rufus, *The History of Alexander* 10.5.19–22, 24 (J. C. Yardley trans., Penguin)

# The struggle for succession

The wars of Alexander had resulted in the conquest of an empire and the imposition of a Greco-Macedonian ruling class upon a diverse population that had hitherto been united under Persian control. Greek was now to replace Aramaic as the official written language of the east, although local tongues would endure – just as regional culture and religion would not be wiped out by the mere change of rulers. But the success of the expedition must be measured by the effectiveness of the process of consolidation rather than the speed of conquest.

In fact, the Macedonian conquest was far from complete, as some areas were only partially subdued and others were bypassed intentionally in a bid to come to grips with the Persian King and to strike at the nerve-centres of the Achaemenid Empire. Pockets of independent or recalcitrant states remained throughout the east: Pisidia, Cappadocia, Armenia are notable examples from the north-western region; the Uxians, who had collected payment from the Persians who crossed their territories, and who had been chased from the invasion route by Alexander, were again asserting their independence in the age of the Successors.

When Alexander the Great died in 323, his Notebooks (*Hypomnemata*) included grandiose plans for the conquest of North Africa and the circumnavigation of the Arabian peninsula, though in truth there was much left to be done in areas that had formerly been subject to, or else a thorn in the side of, the Persian kings. The presence of would-be overlords who were even more alien than the Achaemenids served only to strengthen their determination to resist. Some regions rebelled in Alexander's lifetime, incited by the very Persian officials whom he had appointed as satraps and hyparchs.

The border provinces in the east were disrupted by both the presence of hostile elements on the fringes and a reluctance on the part of their Greek garrison troops to remain there. Upon the premature news of Alexander's death – after the attack on the Mallian town in the Punjab – the Greeks of Bactria and Sogdiana, some 10,000 in number, had entertained hopes of abandoning their outposts and marching back to the west, an undertaking that would have exceeded by far the accomplishment of the more famous Ten Thousand three-quarters of a century earlier. The first attempt in 324 was thwarted at the outset; the second, immediately after Alexander's death, resulted in the slaughter of the majority of these troops through the treachery of Peithon, to whom the suppression of the revolt had been entrusted.

Such was the confused state of the new empire when Alexander returned to Babylon to meet his fated end. Between 323 and 321 (or 320), preparations were made to convey the King's body from Babylon to the oasis of Siwah, where he would rest in the lonely embrace of his divine father Amun. Meanwhile, the centrifugal tendencies were encouraged or repressed by the various factions within the officer corps, as each pursued either a course of separatism or the fruitless attempt to preserve the integrity of the empire.

Here again Alexander had been largely to blame: he had never made adequate provision for the succession, nor did he name an heir or even an 'executor' of his will. Perhaps he had designated Perdiccas as regent, by handing his signet ring to Hephaestion's successor on his deathbed. But

The Lion of Amphipolis. Probably a monument to the Macedonians killed in combat. (Author's collection)

some modern scholars have questioned whether this gesture was ever made, assuming that it was part of the propaganda devised by Perdiccas or his military heir, Eumenes of Cardia.

Certainly, Alexander had been wrong in keeping his officers on a fairly equal footing. This had, perhaps, increased his own security, for, once he had freed himself from the clutches of older generals and their factions, he was not eager to create powerful new rivals. Instead, he balanced one appointment with another, encouraging a certain amount of rivalry and even open confrontation. As a result, the army too was divided, each section favouring its own commander or combination of commanders. An even greater divide existed between the cavalry and infantry. In short, a peaceful and effective transfer of power was all but impossible.

Thus history moves from the age of the brilliant conqueror to that of his Successors (*Diadochoi*). Amongst the first to contest the prize were the young and able officers who were coeval with the King, and who had been raised at the Macedonian court and educated along with the Crown Prince at Mieza. They were also the first to die. Some admittedly endured and established dynasties that would rule the so-called Hellenistic kingdoms – Seleucus, Lysimachus and Ptolemy – but others, like Antipater and Antigonus the One-Eyed, were grisled veterans in 323. The former did not long survive the King. Antigonus, however, lived until 301, when he perished on the battlefield of Ipsus. Many indeed were the companions of Alexander who crossed the threshold of old age, and even then few died in their beds. Ptolemy, son of Lagus, better known as Ptolemy I Soter of Egypt, proved a rare exception.

In the early stages, the struggle was to exercise authority on behalf of inept or illegitimate candidates for the throne, or else to defy such authority in a bid to carve out a portion of the empire for oneself. In the latter group, we find Ptolemy, who from the first chafed at the thought of serving under a fellow officer, and Peithon, a former

*Ptolemy, son of Lagus, ruler of Egypt*
Ptolemy is perhaps one of the best known of Alexander's commanders to the modern reader. Nevertheless, in 323 BC he was far from being the most noble, influential or most accomplished of the King's marshals. Born in the 360s, he was older than many of the other young generals and he may not have held his first command until late 331 (at the Persian Gates); if so, he was what we would call a 'late bloomer'. During the campaigns in what are now Afghanistan and Pakistan, he came into his own as a military commander; he had also been a member of the Bodyguard since 330. When Alexander died, he received the satrapy of Egypt, which he fortified and put on a sound administrative and economic footing. Thereafter it was impossible to dislodge him, and he ruled there until 283, sharing the throne with his son, Philadelphus, in the period 285–283. At some point, he wrote a *History of Alexander*, which is now lost.

Bodyguard. The supporters of the kingship were men like Perdiccas, Aristonous, Eumenes and probably Craterus, but the kings themselves were hardly imposing figures: one was a mentally defective half-brother of Alexander, named Arrhidaeus but known officially as Philip III; the other was the infant son of Alexander and Roxane, hampered as much by his semi-barbarian blood as by his age. And, in the wings, there was Heracles, the illegitimate son of Alexander and his mistress, Barsine, the daughter of the Persian Artabazus and a Rhodian woman.

Matters were made worse by the army's hostility to Alexander's plans to integrate Persians into the military and the command structure. Some accommodation would have to be made with the barbarian if the multicultural empire was to become a cohesive whole. This included also a shifting of the government to a more central location – probably to Babylon, though some have disputed this claim – since it would be impossible to rule the east from Pella.

Hence the *Diadochoi*, starting from a position of disadvantage and weakness, could scarcely be expected to succeed. Posterity remembers them as lesser men who jeopardised the whole for the sake of individual gain, whose pettiness and personal rivalries squandered all that Alexander had won and sacrificed countless lives in the process. This verdict is unfair. Premature death had saved Alexander's reputation, ensured his greatness. His generals were left to clean up the mess, to attempt to consolidate the conquered empire, without enjoying any of the authority of the man who had created it.

The wars of the Successors lasted until the late 280s, when Lysimachus was killed in the battle of Corupedium and his conqueror Seleucus was assassinated by an opportunistic and ungrateful son of Ptolemy Soter known to posterity simply as Ceraunus ('The Thunderbolt'). Then it was that the Successor kingdoms came to be ruled by the offspring of the conquerors: the Hellenistic kingdoms had been formed.

The Antigonids (descendants of Antigonus the One-Eyed and Demetrius the Besieger) ruled Macedon and dominated the affairs of the south by garrisoning the so-called Fetters of Greece – Demetrias (near modern Volos), Chalcis and Acrocorinth. In 197, at Cynoscephalae, Philip V was defeated by the Romans in what is called the Second Macedonian War; a Third Macedonian War, in which Philip's son Perseus succumbed to the army of L. Aemilius Paullus, effectively brought Antigonid rule to an end.

In Egypt the Ptolemaic dynasty enjoyed a period of prosperity in the third century BC, especially under its 'Sun-King', Ptolemy II Philadelphus, but by the late second century it was in decline and threatening to destroy itself from within. An unpopular and weak ruler, dubbed Auletes ('the Flute-Player') by the Alexandrians, survived only with Roman aid, as did his daughter, Cleopatra VII, who linked her fortunes first to Julius Caesar, then to Mark Antony, and thus attained a measure of greatness. Ultimately, however, these associations brought her infamy and the destruction of her kingdom.

The most extensive and diverse territory – that is, the bulk of Alexander's empire – was ruled by the descendants of Seleucus Nicator. Already in his reign, the eastern satrapies were ceded to Chandragupta. In the time of his successor, Antiochus I, the Galatians entered Asia Minor and settled around Gordium and modern Ankara, posing a threat to the Hellenes of Asia Minor, who gradually turned towards the dynasts of Pergamum. The third man of this line, Attalus I, gave his name to the dynasty, which sought the friendship of Rome as a means of protecting itself from the Antigonids in the west and the Seleucids in the east. There were indeed short-term advantages but, in the long run, Roman protection entailed loss of freedom in matters of foreign policy. In 133, when Attalus III died, he left his kingdom to the Romans, who converted it into the province of Asia.

The Seleucids themselves had been crippled by the War of the Brothers in the second half of the third century. A brief reassertion of Seleucid power under Antiochus III proved ephemeral, for in 189 that king met with decisive defeat at the hands of the Romans. The subsequent Peace of Apamea deprived the Seleucids of their lands west of the Taurus Mountains and imposed a huge indemnity upon them. From this point onwards, it was a story of steady decline. Pressured by the Parthians in the east and threatened by a revived Ptolemaic kingdom to the south, the Seleucids embarked upon a series of civil wars between rival claimants to the throne. By the middle of the first century, they had ceased to exist, having been crushed by the competing forces of Roman imperialism, Parthian expansion and Jewish nationalism.

# Further reading

## Ancient sources

Arrian, *The Campaigns of Alexander*, translated by A. de Sélincourt, with notes by J. R. Hamilton, Penguin Classics, Harmondsworth, 1971.

Diodorus of Sicily, translated and edited by C. Bradford Welles, Loeb Classical Library, vol. VIII, Cambridge, Massachusetts, 1963.

Justin, *Epitome of the Philippic History of Pompeius Trogus, Books 11–12: Alexander the Great*, translated by J. C. Yardley, with commentary by Waldemar Heckel, Clarendon Ancient History Series, Oxford, 1997.

Plutarch, *The Age of Alexander*, translated by Ian Scott-Kilvert, Penguin Classics, Harmondsworth, 1973.

Quintus Curtius Rufus, *The History of Alexander*, translated by J. C. Yardley, with introduction and notes by Waldemar Heckel, Penguin Classics, Harmondsworth, 1984.

## Modern works

Berve, H., *Das Alexanderreich auf prosopographischer Grundlage*, 2 vols, Munich, 1926.

Borza, E. N., *In the Shadow of Macedon: The Emergence of Macedon*, Princeton, New Jersey, 1990.

Bosworth, A. B., *Conquest and Empire: The Reign of Alexander the Great*, Cambridge, 1988.

Bosworth, A. B., *Alexander and the East: The Tragedy of Triumph*, Oxford, 1996.

Bosworth, A. B. and Baynham, E. J. (eds), *Alexander the Great in Fact and Fiction*, Oxford, 2000.

Briant, P., *L'Empire Perse de Cyre à Alexandre*, Paris, 1996.

Carney, E. D., *Women and Monarchy in Ancient Macedonia*, Norman, Oklahoma, 2000.

Cook, J. M., *The Persian Empire*, New York, 1983.

Engels, D.W., *Alexander the Great and the Logistics of the Macedonian Army*, Berkeley, California, 1978.

Errington, R. M., *A History of Macedonia*, translated by Catherine Errington, Berkeley, California, 1990.

Fuller, J. F. C., *The Generalship of Alexander the Great*, New York, 1960.

Green, P., *Alexander of Macedon, 356–323 BC: A Historical Biography*, London, 1970; repr. Berkeley, California, 1991.

Hammond, N. G. L., *The Genius of Alexander the Great*, Chapel Hill, North Carolina, 1997.

Heckel, W., *The Last Days and Testament of Alexander the Great: A Prosopographic Study*, Historia Einzelschriften, Heft 56, Stuttgart, 1988.

Heckel, W., *The Marshals of Alexander's Empire*, London, 1992.

Holt, F. L., *Alexander the Great and Bactria*, Leiden, 1988.

Lane Fox, R., *Alexander the Great*, London, 1973.

Marsden, E. W., *The Campaign of Gaugamela*, Liverpool, 1964.

Olmstead, A. T., *History of the Persian Empire*, Chicago, 1948.

Pearson, L., *The Lost Histories of Alexander the Great*, New York, 1960.

Roisman, J. (ed.), *Alexander the Great: Ancient and Modern Perspectives*, Lexington, Massachusetts, 1995.

Sekunda, N. and Chew, S., *The Persian Army 560–330 BC*, Osprey Elite Series, no. 42, Oxford, 1992.

Stein, A., *On Alexander's Track to the Indus*, London, 1929.

Stewart, A., *Faces of Power: Alexander's Image and Hellenistic Politics*, Berkeley, California, 1993.

Stoneman, R., *Alexander the Great*, Lancaster
    Pamphlets, London, 1997.
Warry, J., *Alexander 334–323 BC: Conquest of
    the Persian Empire*, Osprey Campaign
    Series, no. 7, Oxford, 1991.

Wilcken, U., *Alexander the Great*, with notes
    and bibliography by E. N. Borza, New
    York, 1967.
Wood, M., *In the Footsteps of Alexander the
    Great*, Berkeley, California, 1997.

# Glossary

*agema*: the elite guard of the cavalry or the hypaspists.

**archon**: a senior magistrate (literally, 'one who is first', 'one who leads'). Philip II and Alexander were archons of the Thessalian League.

*baivarpatish*: (Persian) commander of 10,000, i.e. a myriarch.

**chiliarch**: commander of a thousand. Also the Persian *hazarapatish*, who could be either commander of a thousand or the most powerful court official.

**Delian League**: A confederacy of Greek states, mainly maritime, organised by the Athenians in 478/7 (after the Persian invasion of Xerxes was repelled). The League had its headquarters on the island of Delos (hence the name) and its members paid an annual tribute called *phoros*, which was collected by officials known as *hellenotamiai* ('stewards of the Greeks'). Within a generation the League had been converted into an Athenian Empire.

*Doryphoroe*: (literally, 'spear-bearers') the bodyguard associated with kings and tyrants.

*gazophylax*: a Persian treasurer or rather guardian of the treasures.

*hazarapatish*: commander of a thousand. Equivalent of the Greek chiliarch.

**hipparch**: a cavalry commander, i.e. a commander of a hipparchy.

**hoplite**: heavily armed Greek infantryman. The hoplite carried a circular shield, wore a cuirass (breast-plate), a helmet which gave additional protection to nose and cheeks, and (normally, but not always) greaves. To be effective the hoplite had to fight in formation, since the overlap of the shields protected the exposed right side of the warrior. The spear became a thrusting weapon rather than a javelin.

**hypaspists**: (literally, 'shield-bearers') the infantry guard of the Macedonian king. Often they formed a link between the *pezhetairoi* and cavalry in the Macedonian line.

*ilarches*: commander of a squadron (*ile*) of cavalry.

*ile*: see *ilarches*.

*ile basilike*: the Royal Squadron. This fought in the immediate vicinity of the king as a mounted bodyguard. Cleitus the Black was its commander.

**Medism**: the Greek term for collaboration with the Persians. Medising was symbolised in the late sixth and early fifth centuries by the giving of 'earth and water' to the Persian King, but any form of friendly intercourse with Persia could give rise to the charge of Medism.

*melophoroi*: (literally, 'apple-bearers') Persian guards, distinguished by apple-shaped spearbutts.

**myriarch**: commander of 10,000 = Persian *baivarpatish*.

**Oath of Plataea**: according to the historian Herodotus, the Greek allies swore an oath before the battle of Plataea in 479 to punish Medisers, especially the Thebes, with destruction, enslavement and confiscation of property, with a tithe from the proceeds to be paid to the god Apollo.

**Peloponnese**: the southern part of European Greece, south of the Gulf and the Isthmus of Corinth.

**Peloponnesian League**: A league of states, mainly but not exclusively (it included the Boeotians) from the Peloponnesus, which was controlled by its military leader (*hegemon*) Sparta. Unlike the Delian League, it had no compulsory, fixed payments.

*pezhetairoi*: the 'foot-companions', the Macedonian heavy infantry.

*proskynesis*: the Persian practice of doing obeisance to their king. It involves bowing and blowing a kiss. The extent of the debasement depends on the status of the individual.

**Pythia**: the priestess of the god Apollo at Delphi.

**Sacred Band**: A Theban unit constituted in the fourth century under the leadership of Gorgidas, it comprised 150 pairs of lovers, in the belief that these would fight more valiantly for each other. It was instrumental in Thebes' major victory at Leuctra (371). The unit was destroyed at Chaeronea (338).

*sarissa*: (sometimes spelled 'sarisa') the Macedonian lance, normally about 15–18ft (4.5–5.5m) for infantrymen and perhaps 14ft (4.25m) for cavalry. In the post-Alexander period it seems to have become longer.

*sarissophoroi*: (literally 'sarissa-bearers') cavalrymen who were armed with the *sarissa*.

**satrap**: governor of a Persian province or satrapy. The Median name *khshathrapavan* means 'Protector of the Realm'.

**satrapy**: see **satrap**.

*Somatophylakes*: the seven Bodyguards of the Macedonian king.

**taxiarch**: a brigade (though some writers call the *taxis* a battalion) commander.

**taxis**: see **taxiarch**.

**Thessalian League**: a political union of the cities of Thessaly, which was normally under the leadership of one of its chief cities, either Pherae or Larisa. Its chief magistrate was originally known as a *tagus*, but later the name was changed to *archon*.

**Trireme**: A warship with three banks of oars (with one man per oar). The type seems to have originated in Phoenicia but was adopted and perfected by the Greeks. The normal complement of the trireme was 200 men.

**xyston**: the cavalryman's spear.

# Index

# Related titles from Osprey Publishing

## MEN-AT-ARMS (MAA)
**Uniforms, equipment, history
and organisation of troops**

## CAMPAIGN (CAM)
**Strategies, tactics and battle experiences
of opposing armies**

## ELITE (ELI)
**Uniforms, equipment, tactics and personalities
of troops and commanders**

## WARRIOR (WAR)
**Motivation, training, combat experiences
and equipment of individual soldiers**

## ESSENTIAL HISTORIES (ESS)
**Concise overviews of major wars
and theatres of war**

## ORDER OF BATTLE (OOB)
**Unit-by-unit troop movements and
command strategies of major battles**
Contact us for more details – see below

## NEW VANGUARD (NVG)
**Design, development and operation
of the machinery of war**
Contact us for more details – see below

**To order any of these titles, or for more information on Osprey Publishing, contact:**
Osprey Direct (UK)  *Tel:* +44 (0)1933 443863  *Fax:* +44 (0)1933 443849  *E-mail:* info@ospreydirect.co.uk
Osprey Direct (USA) c/o MBI Publishing  *Toll-free:* 1 800 826 6600  *Phone:* 1 715 294 3345
*Fax:* 1 715 294 4448  *E-mail:* info@ospreydirectusa.com
**www.ospreypublishing.com**